Scientific Fodder Production

NIPA® GENX ELECTRONIC RESOURCES & SOLUTIONS P. LTD.
New Delhi-110 034

About the Authors

Dr. K. Nalini is a faculty of agriculture in Tamil Nadu Veterinary and Animal Sciences University of Tamil Nadu and specialized in agronomy. She has got 12 years of experience in commercial fodder production in organized livestock farms. She has endowed with teaching and extension service experiences in popularizing fodder production among the veterinarians, students, farmers and farming aspirants. She has published a number of research and popular articles in national and international journals and attended many conferences at national level on fodder production and preservation. Her key areas of interests are fodder production, preservation, mechanized post harvest technologies of fodder production and vermicomposting.

Dr. M. Murugan is Professor of Poultry Science, Tamil Nadu Veterinary and Animal Sciences University of Tamil Nadu. He has got 10 years of working experience in organized livestock farms and especially in fodder production, preservation and integration of animal and agriculture. He has published a number of research and popular articles in national journals and attended many conferences at national level on fodder production and preservation. His key areas of interests are organic fodder production and integrated livestock farming systems.

Scientific Fodder Production

K. Nalini M.Sc. (Agri.), Ph.D.
Assistant Professor of Agronomy
Tamil Nadu Veterinary and Animal Sciences University
Tamil Nadu, India

M. Murugan M.V.Sc., Ph.D. MBA
Professor of Poultry Science
Tamil Nadu Veterinary and Animal Sciences University
Tamil Nadu, India

NIPA® GENX ELECTRONIC RESOURCES & SOLUTIONS P. LTD.
New Delhi-110 034

NIPA® GENX ELECTRONIC
RESOURCES & SOLUTIONS P. LTD.
101,103, Vikas Surya Plaza, CU Block
L.S.C.Market, Pitam Pura, New Delhi-110 034
Ph. +91 11 27341616, 27341717, 27341718
E-mail: newindiapublishingagency@gmail.com
www: www.nipabooks.com

For customer assistance, please contact
Phone: + 91-11-27 34 17 17
Fax: + 91-11-27 34 16 16
E-Mail: feedbacks@nipabooks.com

ISBN: 978-93-58871-26-5

Composed and Designed by NIPA®.

Preface

Firstly, as authors of the book titled Scientific Fodder Production, we raised a question to ourselves that, what is the need of this book and combined authorship of agriculture and veterinary faculties? In India, animal farming is of agriculture based, often called animal agriculture. Forage or fodder crop production is often used synonymously in text books, though they have slight differences in its meaning and application.

Effective production and use of forages is the basis for profitable livestock farming in India where, grains are scarce and costly; forages, fodders, crop residues are relatively cheap for efficient animal feeding regimens. In extensive livestock farming, allowing the animal for grazing is the most cost effective way of feeding, for which good pasture and grazing land management is necessary.

In semi intensive and intensive livestock farming, cultivation of fodder is crucial for cut and carry system and stall feeding to optimize the returns per unit area of use. Combination of cereal, grass, legume fodders with compounded feed is the way of optimizing dietary costs for intensive livestock farming systems of India.

However, in most situations, the importance of fodder in animal farming is under estimated by veterinarians; because, the art fodder production is a part of agriculture domain, many of agricultural institutions are also not offering much importance to the science of fodder production, because the end user of the same are animals maintained by veterinarians.

Even in veterinary colleges, students are least exposed to the science of fodder production and fails to recognize the importance of fodder production in livestock farming. Considering that, issues and complexities of fodder production is often not addressed effectively by both the scientific community in a common platform. To fill up this gap, we planned to write a text book on fodder production with combined expertise.

Fixing the right content for right audience is the first step for successful writing. Student of veterinary and animal sciences, agricultural sciences, livestock farm managers and supervisors, farmers and farming aspirants are the target audience for this book. To feed the audience in a balanced way, we covered the subject in two parts namely, introduction to basic agriculture and introduction to fodder production and related topics of animal feeding.

Introduction to agriculture will expose the students to the basic areas on relationship of agriculture and allied sciences, agro meteorology, agronomical practices, manures and fertilizers, farm machinery etc. Fodder production area will cover the inventory of various fodders, package of practices, preservation, organic fodder production, and integrated farming system. Topics are arranged in a sequential manner with simple, lucid language style with sub titles for easy understanding of the students. Exercises are given at the end of each chapter for practice, and to get a confidence over subject while applying in the field. Interesting topics like labour management in farms, economics of fodder and fodder seed production are presented for effective management of farms.

We strongly believe that, this book on Scientific Fodder Production will serve the purpose by providing a handy and updated scientific knowledge base to target audience and act as teacher cum trainer guide for efficient fodder production. In this juncture, we express sincere thanks to our Tamil Nadu Veterinary and Animal Sciences University for granting permission to write this book. We also express sincere gratitude to our publishers for a quality publishing work. Finally, it is our pleasure to convey thanks to our family members (Manikandan and Narun Sabari; Abbiramy, Muthamil and Manicka) for their lovely moral support.

Place: Tirunelveli **Authors**

Contents

Syllabus

1) Introduction to Agriculture - Importance and scope - Branches of agriculture
2) Agricultural crops and major soils - Soil testing - Introduction to basic agronomical practices - Field preparation -Tillage - Seeds and seed rate - Sowing methods - Planting geometry - Germination - Crop stand establishment - Manures and fertilizers- Irrigation and drainage – Plant protection – Harvesting.
3) Soil moisture conservation practices - Farm machineries.
4) Introduction to agro meteorology - Weather and climate, micro and macro climate Weather elements – Recording of weather data - Monsoon and their influence on different crops - Agro-climatic zones of India.
5) Introduction on forages and fodder – Status of fodder production in India - Types of fodder – Grass, cereal, leguminous and tree fodders, cultivation practices, yield and its nutritive value in animal feeding- Temperate fodder production - Preservation of fodder - Silage and hay - Carrying capacity of farm - Pasture and grass land management - Economics of fodder production - Economics of fodder seed production.
6) Agro forestry and types of agro forestry - Scarcity fodders -Storage of fodders
7) Integrated farming system – Value addition of farm waste - Vermicompost –Panchakavya production - Organic fodder production.

1

Introduction to Agriculture and Allied Sciences

Learning Objectives

- Describe the concept and classification of agriculture and allied sciences
- List the branches of study in agricultural and allied sciences
- Discuss the role of agriculture and allied sciences in Indian economy
- Detail the highlights of Indian agriculture and allied sciences
- Discuss the export potential of agriculture and allied products of India

In broad perspective, agriculture and allied sciences is defined as the art, science and business study of producing crops, livestock, fishery and forestry for food and economic purposes. Considering its broad base of coverage of various items like crop, livestock, fishery and forestry etc., it is generally called as Agriculture and allied sciences. The etymology of the term Agriculture has two Latin words, *Agri* and *Cultura* meaning soil and cultivation. In a holistic sense, agriculture is an applied science comprising of the study of plants and animals like crops, fruits, vegetables, livestock and poultry, fishery, forestry and home sciences etc. It is one the core and primary sector of Indian economy.

Branches of Agriculture

Basically, there are seven broad branches in agriculture and allied sectors namely,

1) Agronomy: It is the scientific study of production of various food, cash and fodder crops. Here, food crops include cereals, pulses, oilseeds etc., cash crops includes sugarcane, cotton, jute etc. and, fodder crops includes various grass, leguminous and cereal crops used for animal feeding exclusively.

2) Horticulture: It is the scientific study of production of fruits, vegetables, flowers, spices, condiments, beverages and ornamental plants etc.

3) Forestry: It is the study of commercial cultivation of trees for producing timber rubber, wood other forest products and agro forestry for related industries.

4) Animal Husbandry: It is the scientific study of breeding and rearing of various livestock and poultry species for food, economic and agricultural purposes.

5) Fishery: It is the scientific study of breeding and rearing various types of fishes in marine and inland water bodies for food and economic purposes.

6) Agricultural Engineering: It is of engineering study of designing and operating agriculture and allied sectors farm machineries, implements and tools for field works.

7) Home Science: It is scientific study of application, utilization, processing and value addition of several products of agriculture and allied sectors, for food and economic purposes.

Out of the seven branches, first three namely agriculture, horticulture and forestry are of crop sciences, fourth and fifth namely animal husbandry and fisheries are of animal sciences and sixth and seven namely agricultural engineering and home sciences are common to both crop and animal sciences.

The minor and specific branches of agriculture and allied sectors are

1) Pomology: Cultivation of fruit bearing trees for food and economic purpose

2) Olericulture: Cultivation of vegetables for food and economic purposes

3) Floriculture: Cultivation of flower and domestic and industrial uses

4) Sericulture : Rearing of silk worms for textile use

5) Apiculture: Rearing of honey bees for production of honey and other products

6) Dairy: Rearing of dairy cattle for food and economic purposes

7) Piggery: Rearing of pigs for food and economic purposes

8) Poultry : Rearing of birds for food and economic purposes

9) Agro forestry: It is integrated cultivation and agricultural crops, fodder and trees for food and economic purposes.

Role of Agriculture and Allied Sciences in Indian Economy

Agriculture plays a vital role in India's economy. Out of total work force of India, 54.6 per cent is engaged in agricultural and allied sector activities and it accounts for 18.6 per cent of the country's Gross Value Added (GVA) for the year 2021-22 at current prices. Considering the importance of the agriculture sector, Government of India and state governments have taken several steps for its overall development in a sustainable fashion.

As per the land use statistics 2018-19 of Government of India, the total geographical area of India is 328.7 million hectares. The net sown area is 139.3 million hectares and gross cropped area is 197.3 million hectares with a cropping intensity of 141.6 percent. The net sown area is 42.37 per cent of the total geographical area. The net irrigated area is 71.6 million hectares, which forms only 20.8 per cent of the total geographical area.

Out of the total rural households of India, 57.8 per cent are engaged in agriculture. The small and marginal holdings put together constituted 86.08 per cent of the total land holdings in 2015-16. The all- India average size of holding is 1.08 ha. Women constitute 30.33 per cent of total cultivators and 40.67 per cent of agriculture labour. Only 13.95 per cent of total operational holdings are operated by women.

Table 1.1: Agriculture and Livestock Production Data – 2021-2022#

Item	Area of cultivation (Lakh hectares)	Production (Million Tones)	Yield (Kg per Hectare)
Agriculture Produce			
Rice	463.79	130.29	2809
Wheat	304.69	106.81	3507
Coarse Cereals	226.52	50.90	2247
Pulses	310.30	27.69	892
Total Food Grains	**1305.30**	**315.72**	**2419**
Oil Seeds	291.67	37.70	1292
Sugar Cane	51.48	431.81	83887
Cotton	119.10	31.20	445
Jute and Mesta*	6.86	10.32	2709

Advance Estimates for the year 2021-2022
Production in million bales, One bale equal to 180 kg
Source: Annual Report- 2022-2023, Department of Agriculture and Farmer's Welfare, Ministry of Agriculture and Farmer's Welfare, Government of India, New Delhi

Animal Produce -2022			
Item	**Production**	**Per Capita Availability**	**Rank**
Milk	221.06 million tonnes	444 grams per day	First
Egg	129.60 billion	95 numbers per annum	Third
Total meat	9.29 million tonnes	6.82 kg per annum	Eighth
Wool	33.13 million kg	-	-
Contribution of livestock sector to Agriculture GVA			30.87 %
Contribution of livestock sector to Total GVA			6.17 %

Source: Basic Animal Husbandry Statistics -2022, Department of Animal and Dairying, Ministry of Fishery, Animal Husbandry and Dairying, Government of India, New Delhi.

Highlights of Indian Agriculture and Allied Sectors

India is the first largest producer of pulses and total pulses production during 2021-22 is 27.69 million tonnes. Total oilseeds production of India during 2021-22 is 37.70 million tonnes and India is the first largest oil seed producer in the world. India is the second largest cane sugar producer after Brazil and the total production of sugarcane in the country during 2021-22 is 431.81 million tonnes. India is the first largest producer of cotton and jute in the World and for the year of 2021 - 2022, production of cotton is 31.20 million bales (170 kg of cotton is a bale) and production of jute is 10.32 million bales (180 kg of Jute is a bale)

The horticulture sector covering fruits, vegetables, root and tuber crops, flowers, aromatics and medicinal crops, spices and plantation crops, which offers better returns per unit of area apart from diversification in agriculture. Horticulture crops cover an area of 26.22 million hectare 2019-20 with a production of about 319.57 million tonnes of produce. The area under fruit crops during 2019- 20 is 6.70 million hectare, with a total production of 100.45 million tonnes. India is the second largest producer of fruits in the World after China and first largest producer in mango, banana, papaya, lemon fruit production.

Interestingly, vegetables constitute about 59.3 percent ofhorticulture production. Vegetables cultivated in an area of 10.32 million hectare as per 2019-20 and total production is 189.46 Million Tonnes. India is the second largest producer of vegetables after China. India is the market leader in production of vegetable of ladies finger. Besides, India occupies the second position in the world in production of potato, tomato, onion, cabbage, cauliflower and brinjal. The per capita availability of fruits is 209.8 gm / person /day in 2019-20 and the same for vegetables is 395.6 gm / person / day. India is a good player in production of flowers, particularly cut flowers, having potential for exports. Floriculture during 2019-20 covered an area of 0.31 million hectare with a production of 2.99 million tonnes of flowers.

India is the largest producer, consumer and exporter of spices and spice products. The total production of spices during 2019-20 was 9.75 million tonnes from an area of 4.14 million hectare. India is the first largest producer of turmeric and ginger. India is also the second largest producer of tea after China. India is the first largest coconut producer in the world comprises of a 34.73 per cent of global production.

Export Potential of Agriculture and Allied Sector's Products

India is a significant exporter of agriculture and allied sector products like basmati rice, rice other than basmati, buffalo meat, fruits and vegetables, spices, cotton, cashew, sugar, honey, dairy and poultry products.

Table 1.2: Major agriculture and allied sectors product export 2021-2022

Item	Export Value (in Crores)	Export (MMT)
Non Basmati Rice	45652.35	17.26
Basmati Rice	26416.54	3.95
Buffalo Meat	24613.24	1.18
Wheat	15840.34	7.24
Maize	7615.42	3.69
Groundnuts	4697.10	0.51
Processed Vegetables	3986.45	0.46
Processed Fruits, Juices & Nuts	3626.08	0.37
Fresh Onions	3432.16	1.54
Cashew Kernels	3377.40	0.08
Guargum	3334.77	0.32
Dairy Products	2928.80	0.11
Other Fresh Fruits	2900.70	0.76
Pulses	2834.29	0.41
Jaggery & Confectionery	2797.85	0.55
Fresh Grapes	2302.16	0.26
Cucumber and Gherkins	1487.30	0.22
Poultry Products	529.80	0.32
Natural Honey	1221.18	0.07
Fresh Mangoes	327.45	0.03

Source: Agricultural and Processed Food Products Export Development Authority (APEDA), Ministry of Commerce & Industry, Govt. of India.

Based on the above table, it is evident that unique products of export of agriculture and allied sectors are Basmati rice, Buffalo meat, Spices, Guargum, Natural Honey etc. and they are the strengths of Indian agriculture in export market.

Activity

1) Collect the data on total area, net sown area, gross cropped area and cropping intensity of India for the current year.
2) Collect the agriculture production data for the last three years from the Annual Report of Department of Agriculture and Farmer's welfare, Government of India, compare the same and offer your comments.
3) Collect the data of top 15 agricultural products in terms of export value and draw your inferences.
4) Highlight the importance of Basmati Rice and Buffalo meat in terms of its export value in international trade.
5) Discuss the role and functions of APEDA in agricultural product export.

Exam Corner

1. What is agriculture and allied sciences?
2. What is agronomy?
3. What is horticulture?
4. What is animal husbandry?
5. What is fishery?
6. What is home science?
7. What is net sown, gross cropped area?
8. What is Pomology, Olericulture, Sericulture
9. What is Floriculture, Apiculture?
10. What is dairy, piggery, poultry?
11. What is agro forestry?
12. What is APEDA?

2

Classification of Agricultural Crops and Soil

Learning Objectives

- Discuss the classification of agricultural crops and plants
- List the various classifications of agricultural crops and plants
- Explain the descriptive classification of crops
- Describe the ecological classification of crops
- Discuss the agricultural classification of crops
- Explain the various soil types of India
- Explain the process of soil sampling of farm fields

In broad perspective, plants and crops of agriculture can be classified mainly based on three criterions namely descriptive, ecological and agronomical. Understanding these basic classifications will help us to study the characteristics of each plant in detail.

Descriptive Classification

In descriptive approach, plants and crops can be classified based on the mode of reproduction, mode of pollination, life span, growth habits and leaf retention property. Sexual and asexual reproducing plants are the two groups based on the mode of reproduction. The sexual reproducing plants are developed from a seed after the union of male and female gametes and asexual plants reproduces through vegetative means and not by male and female gametes.

Based on the mode of pollination, crops are classified as naturally self pollinated, naturally cross pollinated and both self and cross pollinated crops. In the naturally self-pollinated plants, both pollen and embryo sac are produced in the same floral structure or in different flowers but within the same plant. Typical Examples include: rice, most pulses, okra, tobacco, tomato. In naturally cross-pollinated crops, the pollen transfer is done from one flower to the stigma of another flower in a separate plant. Typical examples include, corn and many grasses, avocado, grape, mango, many plants with unisexual or imperfect flowers. In both self- and cross-pollinated crops, plants are largely self-pollinated but varying amounts of cross-pollination also occur. Examples include, cotton and sorghum.

Based on the life span, crops are classified in to three namely annuals, biennials and perennials. Plants which are live for a short period of time, weeks or months / seasons, produce the seeds and ends its life cycle called as annuals (eg: Rice, Sorghum, Cowpea). Plants which requires two seasons for their life cycle is called as biennials and generally first season for growth and second season for producing reproductive parts (eg: Onion and Carrot). The plants that live for a very longer period of time with underground stems, which includes trees and shrubs are called perennials (eg: Trees, Hybrid Napier grass, Cenchrus grass). The perennial plants continue growing and produce seeds year after year from a single plant

Evergreen plants and deciduous plants are the two groups based on the leaf retention property of a plant. The Evergreen plants are those that maintain their leaves throughout the year (eg: pines, palms). The deciduous plants are those which naturally shed off or lose leaves annually for extended periods (eg: Neem and Teak).

Ecological Classification

The plants and crops are classified according to their ecological adaptation and habitat and they are as follows,

1. Aquatic plants: The plants that is adapted to growing in water or waterlogged soil. They grow in submerged, partly submerged or floating conditions.
2. Epiphytic plants: The plants grow above ground on another plant but are not parasitic in nature, deriving only physical support from the host and obtaining nourishment from the air and other sources. The most common epiphytes belong to the pineapple and orchid.
3. Halophytic plants: The plants grow in salty land or under saline conditions and Mangrove vegetation is the classical example for halophytic plants.
4. Lithophytic plants: Plants that is adapted to grow on rocks or in rocky terrain with little humus, absorbing nutrients from the atmosphere, rain, and decaying matter which accumulates on the rocks.
5. Parasitic plants: Plants that grow on another plant from which it takes part or all nourishment from the host plant.

6. Saprophytic plants: The plants that grow on decaying organic matter and have no green tissue like mushrooms
7. Sciophytic plants: Plants that grow in low light intensity or shade like black pepper, coffee.
8. The Terrestrial plants: The plants that grow on land and most of the agricultural crops are terrestrial plant type.
9. Xerophytic plants: Plants that are adapted to water scarce conditions like cacti

Agricultural Classification

In broad sense, based on the nature of crop, its use, cultivation practices crops and plants of agriculture are classified in two namely agronomic or field crops and horticultural crops. However, in agricultural perspective and its use, crops and plants can be classified as follows,

The food crops are the crops primarily grown for the harvesting of any part of the plant which is used as food or processed food product. It consists of cereals, pulses etc.

On the other hand, the non-food crops are mainly consists of cash crops, and their main use is production non food but economic value products like cotton fibre, fodder, tobacco etc.

Here, the staple crop is basically a food crop and it will be consumed by the people regularly in considerable quantities for their daily nutrient requirements like rice, wheat, millets etc.

The cereal or grain crops are mainly annual crops of herbaceous plants, which are grown for their seeds or grains like corn, millet, rice, sorghum, wheat. The legume seed crops or pulses are leguminous plants which produce edible, protein-rich seeds like black gram, bengal gram etc. The root and tuber crops are plants with swollen root or underground stem, which is a rich source of carbohydrate and has multi utilities like, food, livestock feed and other industrial uses. Oil seed crops are plants grown for their seeds which are rich source of edible or inedible oil for industrial use like groundnut, sunflower, gingely, jatropha etc.

The pasture and intensively cultivated forage crops are also special group of plants grown or managed as feed for livestock. Soilage Crops are the grasses grown, cut and directly fed to animals. Apart from the above, sugar crops, beverage crops like coffee, tea, latex producing crop like rubber etc are also available for agricultural production. One of the major divisions in agricultural crops is horticultural crops also as referred to as garden crops. It consists of vegetable crops, fruit and nut crops, spice crops, oil crops, ornamental crops etc.

Soil

The soil is a loose material forms the upper layer of earth formed from the weathering of rock consisting of inorganic and organic particles, air, water and living organisms. It offers structural nutrient support for the plant growth. The major factors that influence the formation of soil are parent material, relief (height differences), climate, vegetation, life forms and time etc. The process of soil formation is called as *Pedogenesis.*

Soil Profile

The soil profile is a vertical cross section of the soil which made of layers parallel to the surface and each layer of soil has a different texture and known as the horizon.

Horizon A (Topsoil)

It is the topmost layer where the organic materials have got mixed with the mineral matter, nutrients, water and elements necessary for the growth of the plants.

Horizon B (Subsoil)

This zone has a greater content of minerals and humus is present in smaller quantities and it represents a transition between Horizon A and Horizon C and contains matter derived from below and as well as above.

Horizon C (Weathered and decomposed rock)

This layer is composed of loose parent rock and it is the base layer for soil formation process forms the above two layers. The material under these three layers is parent rock or bed rock soil.

Soil Types in India

In India, the Indian Council of Agricultural Research (ICAR) has classified soils into eight types namely

1) Alluvial soil
2) Red and yellow soil
3) Black soil

4) Laterite soil
5) Mountaineous or Forest soil
6) Arid or Desert soil
7) Saline and Alkaline soil
8) Peaty and Marshy soil

Alluvial Soils

Alluvial soil is one of the predominant soil types in India and covers around 40 per cent of the total land area of the country. They are widespread in the northern plains and river valleys and it derived from the debris brought down from the Himalayas and in peninsular region, they are found in deltas of the east coast and in the river valleys. The colour of the soil is light grey to ash grey and sandy loamy to clay. Generally they are rich in potash and poor in phosphorus. Alluvial soil is suitable for intensive cultivation of cereals, pulses oil seeds, sugarcane including fodder cultivation.

Red Soil

It is the second largest (18 per cent) soil type in India also considering its colour it is also known as the omnibus group soil. It is commonly found in low rainfall regions of eastern and southern parts of the Deccan Plateau and Western Ghats. This soil is also present in parts of Odisha and Chattisgarh and in the southern parts of the middle Ganga Plain. The red colour of the soil is due to the presence of iron in crystalline and metamorphic rocks. The soil appears yellow when it is in hydrated form. The fine grained red and yellow soil is usually fertile compared to coarse grained soil. This type of soil is generally deficient in nitrogen, phosphorus and humus. Wheat, cotton, oilseeds, millets, tobacco, pulses and fodder are mainly cultivated in red and yellow soil

Black Soil

Black soil is the third largest soil type in India covers around 15 per cent of the land area of the country and it is also known as the Black Cotton Soil. It predominantly covers the most of Deccan Plateau states like Maharashtra, Madhya Pradesh, Gujarat, Andhra Pradesh and some parts of Tamil Nadu. The black soils are generally clayey, and impermeable. They swell greatly and become sticky in the rainy season. In the dry season, the moisture evaporates and the soil shrinks and develops wide cracks. The colour of the soil is deep black to grey. Black soil is rich in iron, lime, aluminium, magnesium and potassium and deficit in nitrogen, phosphorus and organic matter. Cotton is the most suitable crop for black soil, apart pulses, millets, castor, tobacco, sugarcane including fodder crops are mainly cultivated in black soil.

Desert Soil

Desert soil also known as arid soil, it covers about four per cent of the total land area of the country. The colour ranges from red to brown. Desert soils are sandy to gravelly in texture, have low moisture content and low water holding capacity. These soils are saline in nature and in certain regions the salt content is so high that common salt is obtained by evaporating water. Desert soils are very common in western Rajasthan with little organic matter.

Laterite Soil

Laterite soil accounts for about 3.7% of the total area of the country and these are typical soils of the monsoon climate which is characterized by seasonal rainfall. In rainy seasons, lime and silica are leached away, and soil rich in iron oxide and aluminium are left leading to the formation of laterite soil. Laterite soil is deficient in organic matter, nitrogen, phosphate and calcium; however iron oxide and potash are in abundance. Although low in fertility, they respond well to manures and fertilizers. Laterite soils are found in Karnataka, Tamil Nadu, Kerala, Madhya Pradesh and hilly regions of Assam and Odisha. Red laterite soil in Kerala, Tamil Nadu and Andhra Pradesh are well suited for tree crop cultivation like cashew nuts. Laterite soil hardens rapidly and irreversibly on exposure to the air, a property that leads to its use as making bricks in southern India.

Mountain Soil

This type of soil is found in the forest regions where rainfall is sufficient and it is also called forest soil. The texture of the soil depends on the mountain environment where they are found. These soils are coarse-grained in the upper slopes and loamy and silty on valley sides. In the snowbound areas of the Himalayas, these soils undergo denudation and are acidic with low humus content. The soils found in the lower valleys are fertile.

Saline and Alkaline Soils

These soils are almost infertile having high content of sodium, magnesium and potassium and deficit in calcium and nitrogen. The high salt content is mainly because of the dry climate and poor drainage and texture ranges from sandy to loamy. These soils are found in arid and semi-arid areas, and in waterlogged and swampy regions. These soils are mostly found in western Gujarat, deltas of the eastern coast and in Sundarban areas of West Bengal. In the Rann of

Kutch, the south-western monsoon brings salt particles and deposits there as a crust. Seawater near deltas also increases the salinity of the soil. These soils can be reclaimed by improving drainage, by applying gypsum or lime and by cultivating salt-resistant crops like berseem, etc. . These are mainly found in Rajasthan, Haryana, Punjab, Uttar Pradesh, Bihar, and Maharashtra. Sodium chloride and sodium sulphate are present in this soil. It is suitable for leguminous crops.

Peaty and Marshy Soils

These soils are found in heavy rainfall regions with high humidity and support well the growth of vegetation. Peaty soils are heavy, rich in humus and organic matter black in colour and mostly alkaline. These are found in southern Uttarakhand, the northern part of Bihar, and the coastal areas of West Bengal, Odisha and Tamil Nadu.

Soil Testing

Soil sampling is a procedure to collect the representative soil samples from field area to test the soil fertility in soil testing labs to recommend suitable cropping and fertilizers for improving the productivity. Here it is important to highlight that, representative samples of the field area will be the base line of soil testing results, and a non representative samples will make the soil testing results not applicable. Considering that the vital part of soil testing is proper soil sampling and unfortunately it is the most commonly neglected part by the farm managers in the field. The tools required for soil sampling are soil auger or a space, a clean plastic bucket, clean cloth, suitable cloth bag, marker pens and soil information sheet.

Method of Soil Sampling

Firstly, a visual survey of the field area through a field walk should be conducted to observe the colour, texture, slope, cropping pattern etc. Divide the field in area in uniform portions to the tune of one to two hectares for separate sampling and subsequent pooling. Samples should be taken at several locations in sampling area and a zig-zag pattern of sampling will ensure homogeneity. Scrap away surface litter obtain a uniformly thick slice of soil from the surface to the plough depth from each place.

A V-shaped cut to the depth of 15 cms is made with a spade and remove 1 to 2 cm slice of soil. The sample may be collected on the blade of the spade and put in a clean tray or cloth. Collect at least 10 to 15 samples from each sampling unit. Spread the soil evenly and divide it into 4 quarters. Reject two opposite quarters and mix the rest of the soil again. Repeat the quartering and rejecting process till the sample weigh 500 gram and put in a clean cloth bag.

Write the details of the sample in the information sheet like date of collection, name of the sampler, name of the farmer, location of the farm, survey number, previous crop grown, present crop, crop to be grown in the next season, date of collection, name of the sampler etc, and put a copy of this information sheet in the bag. The bag used for sampling must always be clean and free from any contamination.

The points to be considered while soil sampling for testing are as follows,

1) Spade is a satisfactory tool for soft soil sampling but auger may preferred for hard soils
2) Soil samples should not be collected from areas like fertilized field, marshy, old path, old channel, old bunds, area near the tree, site of previous compost piles and other unrepresentative sites of the sampling area
3) Where crops have been planted in rows, collect samples from the middle of the rows so as to avoid the fertilizer effect.
4) Soil samples should be examined for cleanliness as well as for strength before filling up the soil samples
5) Information sheet should be clearly written with copying pencil

Activity

1) Prepare a inventory of plants of your farm based on pollination
2) List the cereal, grass, leguminous, fodder and multipurpose trees of your farm
3) List the evergreen and deciduous trees of your farm
4) Discuss the annual and perennial crops of your farm
5) Discuss the soil types of your farm
6) Take soil samples from different fields for soil testing

Exam Corner

1. What is descriptive classification of plants?
2. What is ecological classification of plants?
3. What is agricultural classification of plants?

4. What is pollination?
5. List some self and cross pollinating plants
6. What are aquatic, epiphytic, halophytic plants?
7. What are saprophytic, parasitic plants?
8. List some cereal crops
9. List some pulse crops
10. List some plantation crops

3

Agricultural Meteorology

Learning Objectives

- Explain the concept of agricultural meteorology and its importance
- Detail the concept of atmosphere, weather, climate and its interactions
- Discuss the various climatic factors of agriculture and its measurements
- Discuss the various seasons of India and its role in agriculture
- Explain the events of flood and drought and its impact in agriculture
- Describe the various agro climatic regions of India

Meteorology is a branch of physical sciences, which studies the physical properties of earth's atmosphere, and it is a combination of physical and geographical sciences. It is an applied science using the principles of physics to understand the physical state and behaviour of atmosphere.

In meteorology, weather describes the physical state of atmosphere of a particular place in a given point of time, usually for a shorter duration. On the other hand, climate describes the state and dynamics of the same set of weather variables of a particular place for a longer period.

Agricultural meteorology shortly known as Agro meteorology is a branch of agricultural sciences, which not only studying the state of atmosphere in terms of physical weather variables, but also study the interaction between the state of atmosphere, environment with the agricultural and allied sectors production practices and systems.

It is trying to forecast the weather of a particular place for a given point of time to plan the agricultural production practices according the weather status to get better production and productivity. It is also forecasting the meteorological abnormalities like cyclones, very heavy rainfall and drought etc., to avoid the losses in the agricultural production systems. Moreover, study of meteorology variables and forecasting the dynamics of the same will be helpful for farmers in planning cropping patterns, sowing time, necessity of irrigation, harvesting time in view of maximizing the crop yield.

Coordinates of India

Coordinates are a unique identifier of a geographic location on the earth, usually expressed in alphanumeric characters. Coordinates are points of intersection in a grid system. Global Positioning System (GPS) coordinates are usually expressed as the combination of latitude and longitude.

Latitude is a measure of degrees of distance from the equator, which is 0 degrees. The north and south poles are at 90 degrees in either direction. The prime meridian is 0 degree longitude and the locations are measured according to 90 degrees east or west from that point. India, the main land is situated north of the equator between 8°4' north to 37°6' north latitude and 68°7' east to 97°25' east longitude.

Atmosphere

The shape of the earth is elliptical and it has three spheres namely hydrosphere (water portion) Lithosphere (solid portion) Atmosphere (gaseous portion). The atmosphere is a colourless, odourless and tasteless physical mixture of gasses which surrounds earth on all sides. It is mobile, compressible and expandable also. It contains huge number of solid and liquid particles called aerosol. The lower part of atmosphere where the chemical composition of gas is uniform is called homosphere. At higher levels the chemical composition of air changes considerably and known as heterosphere.

Atmosphere provides oxygen for respiration of living organisms, carbon-dioxide for photosynthesis, nitrogen for plants growth, rain for plant and animal growth, medium for transportation of pollen etc. It also offers protection from harmful ultra violet rays of solar system.

Gaseous composition of atmosphere	
Nitrogen (N2)	78.08 %
Oxygen (O2)	20.95 %
Argon (Ar)	0.93 %
Carbon di oxide (Co2)	0.03 %
Neon, Helium, Ozone, Hydrogen, Methane	Traces

Atmosphere is divided into different spheres on the basis of vertical temperature variation namely Troposphere, Stratosphere, Mesosphere, Thermosphere and Exosphere, of which study of Troposphere is critical, because, it is the immediate sphere to the living organisms of earth and the largest portion of atmosphere having direct influence on meteorological variables and in turn weather and climate. Hydrological cycle, green house effects etc., are taking place in this sphere only, which are having direct impact on weather and climate. The range of altitude of troposphere is 8-15 kms and decreasing temperature with increasing altitude is the characteristic feature.

Weather

Weather describes the state or condition of the atmosphere of a place at a given point of time in terms of meteorological elements like temperature, humidity, sunshine, wind velocity, rainfall and they are expressed in suitable numerical values. These variables are highly variable in nature from time to time even in a day.

Climate

Climate describes the generalized weather or summation of weather conditions of a given region in a comparatively longer period. It is a sum of all statistical information of weather of a particular area during a specified interval of time, usually, a season or a year or even a decade. It is the study of weather conditions in a given area, characterized by long-term statistics like mean and variable values of the meteorological elements of that area. The climatic values are generally worked out for a period of 30 years often called as climate normal.

Difference between Weather and Climate

Weather	Climate
Describes the physical condition of the atmosphere of a given area at a given point of time	Generalized condition of the atmosphere of a larger region from the analysis of its meteorological values of longer period
Changes and instant from place to place even in a small area	Comparatively constant but different in different large region
Similar numerical values of weather of different places usually have same weather	Similar numerical values of climate of different places usually have different climates
Weather of a given area decides the crop growth, development and yield.	Climate decides the selection of suitable crops for a place or a region

Climate Factors

Latitude

Latitude is the first foremost factor affects the climate. The degree of latitude indicates the distance of a place from the equator (equator is at zero degree) either on south or north and it creates notable variations in the climate of the area. Based on the latitude climate of an area can be classified in to tropical, sub tropical, temperate and polar climate.

Altitude

Altitude indicates the elevation of a place from Mean Sea Level (MSL) and it is also a potential factor of climate variation. Even in the tropical regions, the high mountains have almost temperate climate. The temperature decreases by 6.5 °C / Km rise from the sea level. Apart from that there is also a decrease in pressure and increase in precipitation and wind velocity, which are acting as factors of kind of vegetation, soil types and the agriculture and allied sector production systems.

Precipitation

The precipitation describes the quantity and distribution of rainfall of a particular area due to hydrological cycle which decides the nature of vegetation and agriculture production. The regions are classified on the basis of average rainfall as follows.

Name of the climatic region	Annual Rainfall
Arid	Less than 500 mm
Semi Arid	500-750 mm
Sub Arid	750- 1000 mm
Humid	More than 1000 mm

Soil type

Soil is a particulate product of rocks modified by landscape and vegetation over a long period of time in a given area. The colour of the soil surface is having effect on the absorption, storage and radiation of heat. White colour reflects and black absorbs more radiation. Due to differential absorption of heat energy, variations in temperature are created at different places. In black soil areas, the climate is hot while in red soil areas, it is comparatively cooler due to lesser heat absorption.

Water Bodies

The presence of natural or manmade water bodies like seas, rivers, lakes and ponds affect the climate of the surrounding areas. Climate variation between coastal areas and inland is an example. The movement of air from land to sea and sea to land alter the climate of a particular area. Coastal areas will be more humid than inlands which alter the agriculture and animal production systems.

Topography and Vegetation

The landscape like plain, undulated, slope produces marked change in the climate. This involves the altitude of the place, steepness of the slope and exposure of the slope to light and wind. Kinds of vegetation characterize the nature of climate. Thick vegetation is found in tropical regions, where temperature and precipitation will be high. Basically types of vegetations of a region indicate the nature of the climate of that region.

Classification of Climate

Microclimate in agriculture is the combined climatic conditions recorded in a given small area near the earth›s surface. It includes the climatic variables like temperature, humidity, rainfall, sunshine, wind speed, soil type, soil topography, soil moisture, vegetation, which decides the agriculture production systems. One of critical task of agricultural meteorology in defining micro climate is to study the properties of air near the ground and surface layer of soil. In animal farming systems, record of climate variables within the animal house can also be considered as micro climate. Macro climate: Macro climate deals with the study of atmosphere over large areas of the earth and with the large scale atmospheric motions that cause weather.

Solar Radiation

Sun is the nearest star to the plant earth, and it is the prime source of energy in the form of heat and light for earth. Surface temperature of the sun is around 5500 degree Celsius. The process of receiving radiation from sun by the earth is called as insolation and sun emits energy in the form of electromagnetic waves. The factors affecting insolation are solar constant, energy output of sun, distance of earth from sun, duration of sunlight period, angle of sun's rays etc.

Four processes of heat transfer are conduction, convection and radiation and evaporation.

Conduction is the a process in which, heat is transferred from the hot part to the cold part of the body through the transfer of energy from one particle to another particle of the body without the actual movement of the particles from their equilibrium positions is called conduction and heating a pan in stove is an example.

Convection is the process in which transmission of heat through actual movement of molecules of the medium. It is mostly applicable to liquids and gases. This is predominant form of energy transmission on the earth and all the weather related processes involve this process and the example for the same is boiling of water in a beaker.

Radiation is transfer of energy from one body to another without the aid of the medium (solid, liquid or gas). Radiation heat transfer is a process where heat waves are emitted that may be absorbed, reflected, or transmitted through a colder body. Sun heats the earth by electromagnetic waves through the space is a classical example for radiation of solar energy.

Solar and atmospheric radiation wave lengths for Agro meteorology			
Short wave	UV-C	100-280 nm	Emission from sun and totally absorbed by the atmosphere before reaching the ground
	UV-B	280-315 nm	Emission from sun and 90 per cent absorbed by the atmosphere, biologically very active, causes sunburn
	UV-A	315-400 nm	Emission from sun, biologically not very active
	Visible	400-780 nm	Visible from Violet to Red (colours of rainbow) Very useful for plants growth and called as Photosynthetically Active Radiation
Long wave	Infrared	Above 780 nm	Heat radiation from sun, atmosphere, clouds and surroundings

Temperature and Heat

Temperature is a measure of heat. Heat is the transfer of kinetic energy from one medium or object to another or from an energy source to a medium or object. Such energy transfer can occur in three ways: radiation, conduction, and convection. Heat is often defined as energy in the process of being transferred from one object to another because of the temperature difference between them.

Sensible heat is the heat that can be measured by a thermometer and thus sensed by humans and measured in Celsius, Fahrenheit and Kelvin. Latent heat is the energy required to change a substance to a higher state of matter. This same energy is released on the reverse process. Change of state through evaporation and condensation is known as latent heat of evaporation and latent heat of condensation. For the change of water to water vapour takes 600 calories and water to ice releases 80 calories.

Light

The term light denotes the visible spectrum of the solar radiation and it is one of the vital climatic variables for a plant life. Firstly, it is highly essential for the synthesis of the most important plant pigment Chlorophyll, which absorbs the solar energy for photosynthesis. The intensity, quality, duration and direction of light are important factors for optimum plant growth.

The light intensity is measured by comparing with a standard candle. The quantum of light received at one meter distance from a standard candle is known as Metre candle or Lux. The light intensity at one foot from a standard candle is called foot candle or 10.764 luxes and the instrument used is called as Lux metre.

Very low light intensity reduces the rate of photosynthesis resulting in reduced growth of plants, on the other hand, very high intensity is detrimental to plants and it causes increase in respiration and transpiration rates and rapid loss of water from plants. In response to the light intensity, plants are classified in two namely *Sciophytes* denotes shade loving plants and grow better under partially shaded conditions and *Hetrophytes* are the plants produce maximum dry matter under high light intensities, when the moisture is available at the optimum level like maize, sorghum, rice etc.

In photosynthesis of plants, the main wave length absorbed is violet to blue and orange to red. Among short waves, X rays, gamma rays and long waves such as near and far infrared rays are detrimental to plant growth. Ultra – violet and shorter wave lengths kill bacteria and many fungi.

The duration of light has considerable influence than the intensity of light in canopy development and final yield and plays a important role in selection of crop varieties. The response of plants to the relative length of the day and night is known as phtoperiodism.

In response to the duration of lights, plants are classified as Long day plants, denotes the plants which develop and produce normally, when the photoperiod is greater than the critical minimum 12 hours (eg. wheat, barley) and Short day plants denotes the plants which develop normally when the photoperiod is less than the critical maximum 12 hours. (eg. rice, sorghum, cotton, sunflower) and Day Neutral, those plants which are not affected by photoperiod (eg. tomato, maize).

Air Temperature

Air temperature is defined as the measure of speed per molecule of all the molecules of a body, but heat is the energy arising from random motion of all the molecules of a body. There are number of factors affecting air temperature namely latitude, altitude (density of air and heat absorbing capacity decreases as the altitude increases), nearness of water bodies (variation in land and water body insolation), winds, cloudiness, nature of landscape (plains, mountains and its passes, valleys) and surface etc.

Variation in air temperature is much greater in land than in water. The differential heating process between land and water surfaces are due to their absorbing properties, which is one of the main reasons for Indian monsoons.

Diurnal and Seasonal Variation of Air Temperature

Generally, at the time of sunrise, the minimum air temperature will occur, afterwards, there will be a constant rise till the temperature reaches its maximum and the maximum temperature is recorded at 13.00 to 14.00 (1-2 pm afternoon), though the highest solar radiation occurs at the noon. After the record of maximum, steady fall will happen in the air temperature.

Consequently, a daily chart temperature will have a maximum and minimum point of temperature in a day. The difference between the maximum and minimum temperature of a day is called *diurnal range* of air temperature. In clear days, the range will be very sharp, but on rainy and cloudy days the range will lack its sharpness. It is also affected by season, vegetation coverage etc. Mean of daily maximum and minimum temperature is daily mean temperature.

In horizontal air temperature distribution, the lines connecting points of equal temperature is called as *Isotherms*, which largely depends on latitude. A general decrease in temperature from equator towards poles is one of the fundamental factors of climatology. Distribution of land mass and water bodies on earth's surface alter the latitudinal variation in temperature as land areas warm and cool rapidly than water bodies. Mountain barrier also influence the horizontal distribution of temperature. In vertical air temperature distribution, as the altitude increases, temperature will decrease is a normal phenomenon. At times, there may be abrupt increase in temperature as the altitude increases is called temperature inversion, which is mainly due to the reversal of normal heat gradient of the atmosphere. The effects of temperature inversion are cloud formation, precipitation and fog formation in the ground areas.

The minimum threshold temperature is the temperature below which no growth of plants will takes place. Usually it ranges from 4.5 to 12.5 degree C for different crops (Most commonly used value is 6.0°C). Thermal death point is the temperature at which the plant cell will die and normally thermal death point temperature ranges from 50-60 degree C. This varies with plant species. The aquatic and shade loving plants are killed at comparatively lower temperature of 40 degree C.

Air Temperature in Crop Production

Air Temperature strikingly influences the distribution vegetation and it influences all stages of growth and reproductive phases of the crop. It also affects the respiration, and metabolism, leaf production, flowering, diffusion rates of gases and liquids, bio chemicals and enzyme functions of plants. Majority of the higher plants grow between 0 degree C – 60 degree C and crop plants are further restricted from 10 – 40 degree C, however, maximum dry matter is produced between 20 and 30 degree C. Pests and disease attack will be high in high temperature and high humidity seasons. Majority of the crops have upper and lower limits of temperature below or above which, they may not grow well and a desirable temperature when the crop growth is maximum is called cardinal temperature and different crops have different cardinal temperatures.

Soil Temperature

In crop growth, soil temperature is also one of the influencing factors. The roots of plants, beneficial micro organisms and even the sown seeds till the time of germination live in the soil. The physio-chemical and all the essential life processes of plants are also affected by the soil temperature directly. In low soil temperature germination is inhibited and water intake of root is reduced. In a similar way extreme soil temperatures injures plant and its growth is affected. The soil temperature influences many processes of plant growth like germination, development of root system, water and nutrient intake, soil microbial activities, uptake of water, nutrients, mineralization of organic forms of nitrogen etc.

Factors of Soil Temperature

The heat of the ground surface is spread downwards in a wavy form and rate of spread decrease with depth. Factors of soil temperature can be classified in to two namely meteorological and soil factors. The meteorological factors include solar radiation, wind, rainfall, evaporation (coolness) and condensation (heat) of soil moisture. Among all, solar radiation is the primary factor for soil temperature. The soil factor includes soil texture, aspect and slope of the soil, tillage and tilth, organic matter of the soil, soil colour and moisture etc.

The ideal time to measure soil temperature is the growing season (June, July, August) to reflect soil health and ideal time of a day is 1 and 2 p.m. The desirable depth is 4 inches below the soil surface in bare soil location. There are two types of variations observed in soil temperatures namely daily and seasonal. The factors of daily soil temperature variations are depth of soil, diurnal temperature, cooler or sunny day, soil moisture etc. Seasonal factors include, season itself, depth of soil, vegetation and soil texture.

Generalized dynamics of soil temperature and plant growth	
Temperature	**Action**
Ideal soil temperature for planting, plant growth and nitrification is 65 to 86 degree F	
70 degree F	Hundred per cent soil moisture used for plant growth
90 degree F	Plant growth slows
100 degree F	Fifteen per cent moisture used for growth and Eighty five percent loss through evaporation and transpiration
115 degree F	Bacteria will start die
130 degree F	Hundred per soil moisture is lost through evaporation and transpiration
140 degree F	Most of the soil bacteria will die

Atmospheric Pressure

The atmospheric pressure or air pressure is the weight of the air, which exerts pressure vertically above a unit area of earth with a central point. In general, the weight of the air presses down the earth with the pressure of 1013 hpa (hector Pascal). Variations in heating of the earth and atmosphere by the sun and rotation of the earth will cause variations in atmospheric pressure or air pressure.

Isobars are defined as the imaginary lines connecting two places of earth having same atmospheric pressure or air pressure. Variations in the atmospheric pressure are classified in two namely diurnal pressure variation and seasonal pressure variation. Diurnal pressure variation is mainly due to expansion and contraction of air due to variations of radiation in a day. Seasonal air pressure variations mainly occur due to variation in the amount of insolation in various seasons and it will be more prominent in tropical regions (equator) than Polar regions. The main factors for atmospheric pressure variations of a given area are temperature, altitude, vapour content of the air.

Wind

In simple terms, the wind is moving air. It is natural that air will move from high pressure area to low pressure area. The movement of air may be horizontal or vertical; mostly wind is horizontal motion of air in the atmosphere. Vertical movement of air will occur occasionally and negligibly, but that vertical movement of air too causes significant weather changes like cloud formation and rain.

The winds have some positive and negative effects on growth of plants. The positive effects of wind on plant growth are transport of heat, pollination and dispersal of seeds, soften the humidity stress and mild wind will be useful for cleaning agricultural produce etc., and the strong and dry wind causes excessive water loss, physical damages to the plants and soil erosion.

The primary factor for all winds is variations in the atmospheric pressure in different areas, mainly due to variations in the solar radiation and heating of earth. Wind speed and direction are also modified by seasonal variation in solar radiation and differential heating processes.

In general wind speed is measured by Anemometer in an open terrain at three meters height of above the ground. Mean daily wind speed is value is average of a day's wind speed values. In the same way, monthly and annual wind speed values can also be calculated from the daily values. Wind direction indicates the direction from which wind comes in is also called as windward direction, and the opposite is called as leeward direction. Wind vane is the instrument used for recording the wind direction. When wind blow more frequently from one direction that is called as prevailing wind direction.

Humidity

The quantum of water vapour that is present in the atmosphere is known as atmospheric moisture or humidity and the actual mass of water vapour present in a given volume of moist air is called absolute humidity, expressed as grams of water vapour per cubic meter or cubic feet. Specific humidity is nothing but weight of water vapour per unit weight of moist air. It is expressed as grams of water vapour per kilogram of air. Mixing ratio is the ratio of the mass of water vapour contained in a sample of moist air to the mass of dry air. It is expressed as gram of water vapour per kilogram dry air.

However, in meteorological and agro meteorology studies, the most used term for humidity measure is relative humidity. It is defined as the ratio between the amount of water vapour present in a given volume of air and the amount of water vapour required for saturation for that volume of air under fixed temperature and pressure and expressed in percentage. This is the most used and practically applicable humidity measure in the agriculture meteorological reports.

In other terms it indicates the ratio of the air's water vapour content to its maximum water vapour capacity at a given temperature expressed in percentage and it gives only the degree of saturation of air and the relative humidity of saturated air is 100 per cent. It is not independent measure, as it affected mainly by temperature. As the temperature increases saturation capacity of the air will also increase will change the dynamics of relative humidity.

There are lot of differences between absolute and relative humidity. The equator will have the highest absolute humidity and minimum at the poles. At the sunrise of the day, absolute humidity will be minimum and maximum at 2 to 3 pm. On the other hand, relative humidity will be maximum at sunrise and minimum at 2 to 3 pm of a day.

Influence of Humidity on Crops

The humidity is not an independent weather factor. It is closely related to temperature, rainfall and wind. Firstly, temperature and humidity decides the crops to be grown in an area. It is a influencing factor on water potential of the plants, controls transpiration and evapotranspiration there by water requirement of plants. The harmful effects of high humidity are the growth of parasite, fungi, bacteria and pests attack on plants. The desirable humidity for majority of the crops is around 40 per cent.

Cloud

In meteorology, a cloud is an aerosol consisting of a visible mass of miniature liquid droplets, frozen crystals, or other particles suspended in the atmosphere. Clouds are an aggregation of minute drops of water suspended in the air at higher altitudes. Based on the positional height and appearance of the cloud, they have classified in four families and in to their sub categories and four families are A, B, C, D.

Family A are high clouds and range is 7 -12 km height. Three sub categories are Cirrus, Cirrocumulus and Cirrostratus and the common feature is ice crystals will be present in this type cloud and does not produce much rain.

Family B clouds are medium height and range is 2.5 to 7 km has two sub categories namely Altocumulus looks called as sheep flock clouds and Alto stratus in which rain and ice will be found in separate entity, give rain in middle and high altitudes.

Family C clouds are low height clouds and range from ground to 2.5 km, which is having three categories namely Strato cumulus, composed of water, Stratus composed of water commonly seen in winter season and Nimbo stratus consists of water and ice crystals which offer steady precipitation.

Family D clouds are formed due to vertical raise of air and its development is mostly due to convection and has wide height range of 0.5 to 16 km. It has two sub categories namely Cumulus composed of water with flat base appearance and Cumulonimbus in which upper and lower level will have ice and water respectively. It will produce speedy winds, thunder storms, lightening especially during summer.

Precipitation or Rain

Rain is the process of precipitation of water particles in the form of drops having diameter greater than 0.5 mm or as smaller widely scattered drops. When the precipitation process is active, the lower air will be moist and the clouds are very deep, rainfall will be in the form of heavy downpour. At times, falling water drops will completely evaporate before reaching the ground too.

Drizzling is uniform precipitation composed of fine drops of water having diameter less than 0.5 mm size and seems to be floated in the air. If the drops in a drizzle completely evaporates before reaching the ground, the condition is referred to as mist.

Snow is the precipitation of white and opaque ice grains and it is the precipitation of solid water mainly in the form of ice crystals. In winter, when temperatures are below freezing in the whole atmosphere, the ice crystals falling from the clouds do not melt and reach the ground as snow.

Hail is the precipitation of pieces of ice with diameter ranging from 5 to 50 mm or more is known as hail and they are relatively common in tropics in the months of March to May. Isohyets are the lines connecting locations, having an equal amount of precipitation.

Monsoon Rainfall Variability

Monsoon is the phenomenon which offers rain fall to India and it consists of number of depressions and cyclones that arise mostly in the Indian Ocean. The cyclones moves towards northeast direction and enter the peninsular India along its west coast and they usually occur in the months of June to September and called South West monsoon or summer monsoon.

A second rainy season from October to December called North East monsoon, in which wind flows from North East. Apart, we are also having summer (Southern India) and winter (Western India) seasons. Out of the four seasons, South West monsoon is the most important, as it contribute around 75 per cent of the total rainfall of the country, however regional variations exists between states depending the on the location and its closeness to sea etc.

The term monsoon indicates the climate connected with the seasonal flow of wind from sea to the land and in summer and land to the sea in winter and though the monsoons are natural happenings in tropical areas, flow of winds is one of the strongest reasons in India for the seasonal rainfall.

South - West Monsoon

The large land mass of north of Indian ocean becomes extremely hot, when sun shines vertically over the Tropic of Cancer in the months of April and May and it creates intense low pressure causing flow of winds from sea to land. The South West monsoon arrives on the Kerala coast on around June 1st and moves quickly through Mumbai and Kolkata between around 15th June and it occupies the entire sub continent in the mid of July. The begin of rainfall will be abrupt during the South West monsoon season and monsoon will arrive at coastal areas like Kerala, Karnataka, Goa and Maharashtra at first week of June and interior parts at July. The South West monsoon wind is divided in to namely the Arabian Sea and Bay of Bengal branches.

North-East Monsoon

The North East monsoon enters India from the northeast and the wind blows from the sea to the land. In general the Northeast monsoon is **limited to**

South India, bringing rain to Tamil Nadu, Puducherry, Karaikal, Yanam, Andhra Pradesh, Kerala, Mahe, and south interior Karnataka from October to December. Low-pressure systems, depressions, and cyclones cause the associated rainfall.

Around sixty per cent of India's net arable land is dependent on rainfall for agriculture, which highlight the importance of monsoon for Indian agriculture. The monsoon is responsible for approximately 70 per cent of India's annual rainfall and determines the yield of a variety of grains and pulses, including rice, wheat, and sugarcane. Monsoonal Rainfall aids in the storage of water for irrigation, electricity generation, and drinking.

Drought

A drought is an unusually persistent dry weather period that is long enough to trigger serious problems such as crop damage and or water supply shortages. Droughts are generally caused by low precipitation over an extended period of time. It is also condition in which crops fail to mature because of insufficient supply of water through rains and in which the amount of water required for transpiration and evaporation by crop plants in a defined area exceeds the amount of available moisture in the soil. In general drought in slow in onset. In broad perspective, drought can be classified in to three namely

Meteorological drought in which annual rainfall is significantly short to the tune of 75 per cent of the climatologically expected normal rainfall over a wide area, then the situation is called meteorological drought. Here, climatologically expected normal rainfall is basis for planning the cropping pattern of a particular area is the point to ponder.

Hydrological drought is a situation in which the hydrological resources like large and small rivers, streams, reservoirs, lakes and ponds like water bodies and wells etc., dry up because of marked depletion of surface water and water table of the particular area will also get affected. The prolonged meteorological drought is the predisposing factor of hydrological drought.

Agricultural drought is condition in which, there will be lack of rainfall and followed by soil moisture deficit to the tune that soil moisture fails to meet the water demand of crops for its growth results in retarded growth and yield. Depending on the time of impact agricultural drought can be classified in to early, mid and late season drought.

Flood

Flood is described as an overflow of water that submerges land that is otherwise usually dry. It is chiefly due to the expected or unexpected very heavy precipitation and it is one of the natural and common weather event. Occurrence of flood may also be rapid or slow, which depends on intensity of rainfall and drainage rate. In general floods can be classified in to three types namely, River flood, Coastal flood, Inland flood. Depending on the speed of occurrence it can be classified in to rapid flood (flash flood) and slow flood.

River flood is flow of the water in a river beyond its capacity of flowing or over the top of the river banks and water may pass on the lands adjacent to the river banks too. It may happen small to large rivers all over the world. The main causes are excessive precipitation for extended period or very heavy precipitation in a short spell of rainy season.

A coastal flood described as the inundation of normally dry land areas along the coast with seawater and it is mainly due to very heavy storms, tides and Tsunami like natural events.

An inland flood is described as sudden flood and water stagnation in the land, otherwise normal and it is mainly due to heavy rain fall in short span of time or lack of drainage too.

Rapid or flash flood is described sudden onset of flood due to very intense rainfall in very short spell of time usually 3-6 hours and rain fall rate and duration decides the rapidity of flood. In flash flood, the scope of drain may not be useful in most situations. The critical reasons for flooding are heavy rainfall, over flowing rivers, break in river banks, dams, canals, ponds, storm rains, lack of vegetation and drain and melting of snow etc. Flooding of agricultural fields is mainly due heavy rain fall, over flowing river and canals, break in river banks, lakes, ponds and other water bodies. It is causing crop destruction completely and making economic losses to the farmers and country.

Climatic Normal

Climatic normal describes about the average value of thirty years of a particular weather variable. Average temperature or relative humidity or rainfall of a particular area for a period of thirty years and it may be weekly, monthly and yearly averages. The crop selection, distribution, production and productivity are depending on the climatic normal of a place in question. Selection of a crop based on climatic normal and climatic requirement of the crop for particular regions will maximize the crop productivity.

Weather Forecast

Prediction of weather for future is Weather Forecast and it may be very short range (0-12 hours), Short range (0-72 hours), Medium range (3-10 days) and Long range (More than 10 days, for a month or a season). Here, Very short range and short range mainly forecasting rainfall, storm etc and will be useful for general public, farmers, fisherman, off shoring work personnel etc. Medium range is mainly forecasting rainfall, heat and cold waves etc. Long range forecasting the seasonal weather profile.

Seasons of India

India Meteorological Department (IMD) classified the whole year in to four seasons based on pattern rainfall and temperature namely,

Sl.No	Name of the season	Months	Agricultural Season
1	South West Monsoon	June to September	Kharif crop season
2	North East Monsoon	October to November	Rabi crop season
3	Winter	December – January	
4	Summer	March, April, May, June	

In hot and humid tropics and sub tropics incidence of pest and disease on plants is substantial. At times it mounts severe restrictions on the distribution and productivity of plants in this region. The highlighting note is the geographical distribution of pests is mainly based on climatic actors especially temperature, humidity, rainfall and wind. Based on the dynamics of these weather variables, incidence of pest and disease attach is also seasonal and periodic. Insect pest outbreaks occur as a result of congenial weather conditions, which facilitate their un-interrupted multiplication and spread. If the occurrence of pest and diseases is predicted in time and space with reasonable accuracy on the basis of relevant weather parameters, suitable and timely preventive and control measures may be scheduled for crop productivity maximization.

Recording of weather data	
Weather Variable	**Method of Recording**
Temperature (Degree Celsius)	Temperature is recorded by using Mercury Thermometer. Generally, temperature is recorded at Morning 8 AM and Afternoon 2 PM in Centigrade (metric) or Fahrenheit.
Maximum and Minimum Temperature (Degree Celsius)	Maximum and Minimum temperature of a day is recorded using Maximum and Minimum Thermometer and the same will be reported in the next day.
Relative Humidity (Per cent)	Relative humidity is recorded using Dry and Wet Bulb Thermometer. Dry and Wet bulb reading will be recorded and difference is Wet bulb depression. Relative humidity will be estimated using Psychometric charts (Relative Humidity charts) by using dry bulb reading and wet bulb depression values and expressed in per cent.

Recording of weather data	
Weather Variable	**Method of Recording**
Rain fall (millimeter)	Rainfall is recorded using standard and calibrated Rain Gauges and expressed in millimeters (mm). Generally, the value will be recorded at 8 AM of every day and that indicates previous day's (last 24 hours) rain fall. Rainfall of 2.5 mm per day is considered as a rainy day.
Air Velocity (Km per Hour)	Wind speed is measured using Anemometers and expressed in Km per Hour.
Soil Temperature (degree Celsius)	Soil temperature is measured using soil thermometer at 15 cm depth of the soil.

Agro Climatic Regions of India

Climate is one of the critical factors which influence the agricultural production of a region and it plays an important role in deciding crop physiology there by creating diversity agricultural production. As per The Planning Commission of India and National Remote Sensing Agency, India has been divided in to various agro climatic zones based on its soil and climate variables like soil type, rainfall, temperature and water resources. There are 15 major agro-climatic regions in India.

The Western Himalayas

This region consists of Jammu and Kashmir, Himachal Pradesh and Uttarakhand with variation in topography like mountains, valleys and slope lands. High variation in summer and winter temperature prevails, with the mean annual rainfall of 750-1500 mm, except in very high altitudes. It is bestowed with number of perennial rivers, with the cultivation of rice, wheat, barley like cereals, tomato, brinjal, chilli, cucumber like vegetables and fruits like apples, peach, pears, almond and walnut.

The Eastern Himalayas

The region consists of Sikkim, Darjeeling hill areas of West Bengal, Assam Hills, Arunachal Pradesh, Nagaland, Manipur, Mizoram, Tripura and Meghalaya, with a undulated topography, sharp slopes, dense forests and speedy rivers. Climate is sub humid with annual rainfall of 2000 mm. Rice, maize, potato like vegetables are main crops, tea plantation at hilly slopes.

The Lower Gangetic Plains

This region covers eastern part of Bihar, West Bengal and Brahmaputra valley in Assam with alluvial soil type due to the deposits of rivers. Topography characterized by slopes and lakes, has humid climate with the annual rainfall of 1000-2000 mm. Marsh lands are characteristic of this region, land suitable for rice, wheat and jute cultivation.

The Middle Gangetic Plains

It covers over eastern part of Uttar Pradesh and whole of Bihar with a gentle sloping plain, alluvial soil. Climate is hot and humid with the annual rainfall of 1000 to 1500 mm. Major crops are rice, maize, millets, mustard, potato, mango, banana etc.

The Upper Gangetic Plains

This stretches over the Ganga-Yamuna doab (flat alluvial soil land), Lucknow division and Rohilkhand of western Uttar Pradesh and areas in Uttarakhand. It is sub humid in climate with the annual rainfall of 750-1500 mm. It is an intensive agricultural region, where wheat, rice, sugarcane, millets, maize, pulses, gram, barley, oilseeds and cotton are widely grown and main targeted area for green revolution.

The Trans-Ganga Plain

The Trans Ganga plain consists of Punjab, Haryana, Delhi, Chandigarh and parts of Rajasthan with semi arid climate and annual rainfall is 400 to 1000 mm.The region has productive alluvial soil. Due to river supply canal and well irrigation is popular and most of the initiatives of Green Revolution carried over here because of soil fertility and sub soil water levels.

Eastern Plateaus and Hills

This area covers the Chotanagpur plateau, Rajmahal Hills and Chhattisgarh plains with red and yellow soils, with patches of laterites and alluviums. Rainfall range is 750 to 1500 mm per annum. Relatively water scarce area, where is rainfed agriculture is dominant rice .maize, millets, mustard, tobacco are main crops.

The Central Plateaus and Hills

This region covers over eastern part of Madhya Pradesh and adjoining parts of Rajasthan, which include parts of Bundelkhand, Malwa Plateau and Vindhyanchal hills, characterized by semi-arid climatic conditions where annual rainfall varies from 500-1000 mm and water scarce region. The soils are mixed red, yellow and black types and wheat, millet, pulses, cotton and sunflower are popular crops.

The Western Plateaus and Hills

This region covers over the southern part of Malwa plateau and the Deccan plateau of Maharashtra and a region of black soil with semi arid climate and rainfall of 250 to 750 mm per annum. Water scarcity is intense with predominant rainfed agriculture. Millets, sugarcane, rice, pulses are main crops.

The Southern Plateaus and Hills

It consists of southern Maharashtra, Karnataka, Telangana, Andhra Pradesh and northern Tamil Nadu with semi arid climate and 500 -1000 mm annual rainfall. Predominantly dry land farming with the production millets, oil seeds, pulses, coffee, tea and cardamom. Animal husbandry and horticulture is popular in this region.

The East Coastal Plains and Hills

The region extends from eastern coast from Odisha to Kanniyakumari of Tamil Nadu and northern part is called Circar and southern part called Coromandel coast. This area is called as Delta because of its formation by depositional works of Mahanadi, Godavari, Kaveri, and Krishna rivers, sub humid in nature with the annual rainfall of 750 – 1500 mm. The main crops are rice, jute, tobacco, sugarcane, maize, millets, pulses, groundnut and oilseeds

The Western Coastal Plains and Western Ghats

The region extends from Tapi Estaury in north to Kanniyakumari in the south and covers coastal areas of Maharashtra, Karnataka and Kerala, northern part is called Konkan and southern part is called Malabar. The mean annual rain fall is 2000 mm and main crops are rice, coconut, millets, pulses and cotton.

The Gujarat Plains and Hills

This region covers the plains and hills of Kathiawar and the fertile valleys of Mahi and Sabarmati rivers with arid and semi arid climate, rainfall 500 -1000 mm per annum. Black and alluvial soils are common in plateau and coastal plains. Groundnut, cotton, rice, oil seeds are main crops.

The Western Dry Region

This region covers over the western part of Rajasthan (west of the Aravalli Hill Range) with arid climate and rainfall is 250 mm per annum. Temperature extremes and sandy desert soil are characteristic features. Millets are main crops and livestock activities are a promising source of income in this area.

The Island Region

The region consists of Andaman and Nicobar Island Bay of Bengal and Lakshadweep Islands of Arabian Sea, with equatorial climate and mean annual rainfall of 2000 mm. Sandy to clayey soils are common and rice, wheat, millets, coconut are major crops.

Activity

1) Record the maximum and minimum temperature, relative humidity, wind speed and rainfall of a day of your farm
2) Collect the weather data of your farm for an year, work out the monthly averages for the same and offer your comments
3) Collect the rainfall data of your farm workout the following and draw your inferences,
    a. Mean monthly rainfall
    b. Total rainfall in South West monsoon
    c. Total rainfall in North East monsoon
    d. Number of rainy days in each monsoon season
    4) Record the soil temperature of minimum six fields of your farm at various seasons and offer your comments.
5) Collect the data on the climatic profile of agro climatic region of your farm location

Exam Corner

1. What is agricultural meteorology?
2. What is the gaseous composition of atmosphere?
3. What is the significance of troposphere?
4. Difference between weather and climate
5. List the factors affecting climate?
6. What is micro climate?
7. What is diurnal variation of air temperature?
8. What is relative humidity?
9. What is drought?
10. What is flood?

11. What is weather forecast?
12. List the monsoons of India
11. List some cash crops
12. What is fodder crop?

4

Agronomical Practices

Learning Objectives

- List the basic agronomical practices in agriculture
- Explain the method of field formation and tillage
- Discuss the methods of sowing of various crops
- Explain the process of germination of plants and crops
- Detail the various methods of irrigation and drainage of soil
- Describe the manuring and harvesting procedure in fodder production

Agronomical practices is the collection of operations starts from field formation, tillage, sowing, irrigation, manure and fertilizer management, pest control and harvest etc. Though, the type of agronomical practices varies with the crop, the basic function of various agronomical operations remains the same for all the crops. Considering that, understanding the basics of general agronomical practices is crucial for good agricultural practices and optimum production.

Tillage

Tillage is the basic activity of preparing the land for the crop production. It is process of mechanical manipulation of soil with tools and implements to bring about a favorable condition of soil for crop production. The process of making soil suitable for agriculture use is called as tillage and well prepared soil is called tilth. In tillage process, the tillage implement, mostly ploughs will open or cut the compact soil surface to a certain depth, lift and turn the soil upside down thereby loosen the soil mass so as to enable the roots of the crops can easily penetrate and spread into the soil. The objectives of tillage are making the soil structure suitable for cultivation, removal of weeds, minimization of soil erosion, mixing of manures and fertilizers etc.

Classification of Tillage

Tillage operation can be classified in two namely Primary tillage and Secondary tillage. Primary tillage is process of using heavy implements to cut open the soil to reduce the soil strength, to remove any weed like plant materials in the land and rearrange soil aggregate. The implements used for primary tillage are called as primary tillage implements. It includes animal drawn and tractor drawn implements like country plough or iron plough, mould-board ploughs, disc ploughs, chisel ploughs and other similar implements.

Secondary tillage is the process breaking the heavy clods produced by the primary tillage and to make a loose and fine structured soil conducive for crop sowing and planting. Secondary tillage also includes the application of manures. The secondary tillage implements are harrow, cultivators, sweeps, levellers, bund formers, ridge ploughs etc.

Sowing of Seed

Seed sowing is the one of the basic step in crop cultivation and it is dependent on the crop geometry of the crop. Recommended plant geometry and right seed sowing depth will improve the possibility of getting maximum yield in any crop.

Seed Rate

Seed rate is the quantity of seed required for sowing or planting in a unit area. The seed rate for a particular crop would depend on its seed size (test weight), its desired population, germination percentage and purity percentage of seed etc. It is calculated as

$$\text{Seed rate (kg)} = \frac{\text{Area to be sown in m}^2 \text{ X Test weight of the seed X 1}}{\text{Germination (\%) X Purity (\%) X Spacing (m) x 1000}}$$

The seed rate per unit area depends on germination of the seed, size of the seed, growing habit of the crop, etc. Higher or lower than the recommended seed rate will affect the plant population, growth and then yield of crop. The seed rate is primarily governed by desirable stand of the crop. Seed rate for irrigated farming will be higher than dry land farming for the same crop.

Seed treatment

Seed treatment is a process of applying or mixing or coating or soaking in solutions of chemicals or protectants with fungicidal, insecticidal, bactericidal, nematicidal or biopesticidal properties, nutrients, hormones or growth regulators to facilitate the easy sowing, germination, protection against pest and diseases etc.

Methods of Seed Treatment

Hot water Treatment

In hot water treatment of seeds, water is boiled to a temperature 80 to 100 ^{0}C and the seeds are soaked in hot water for 3-4 minutes and immediately the water should be drained and washed with cold water for shade drying before sowing. It is highly suitable for hard coat seeds like fodder seeds of Desmanthus spp.

Seed Scarification

Acid Treatment

Acid scarification is the process of dipping the seeds on concentrated sulphuric acid for three minutes and washing thoroughly in tap water

Difference Between Sowing and Planting

Sowing is the placing of a specific quantity of seeds in the soil for germination and growth. Planting is the placing of vegetative / plant propagules (seedlings, cuttings, rhizomes, slips, tubers etc.) in the soil to grow as crops.

Methods of Sowing

Basic methods of sowing are broadcasting, dibbling, drilling, planting, transplanting.

Broadcasting

It is the method of throwing or spreading the seeds in the field and the seeds are closed by the soil by plouging implements. The advantage is simple and more area coverage per unit of time and cost. The disadvantage is that crops will not evenly grow even in fine broad casting.

Dibbling

It is placing of seeds in a hole or pit made at a fixed spacing and depth with a dibbler or planter or by hand. Dibbling is a time consuming and expensive when compared to broadcasting, but it requires less seeds and, gives rapid and uniform germination with good crop geometry.

Drilling

It is a practice of dropping seeds in a definite depth, covered with soil and compacted. Sowing implements like seed drill or seed cum fertilizer drill are used. Manures, fertilizers, soil amendments, pesticides, etc. may be applied along with seeds. Seeds are drilled continuously or at regular intervals in rows. It is time, energy, and cost consuming, but maintains uniform plant population per unit area of cultivation.

Planting

Planting is the process of placing seed or seed material firmly in the soil to grow.

Transplanting

Transplanting is the process of planting seedlings in the main field after pulling out from the nursery. Proper nursery maintenance is mandatory for transplanting will reduce the duration of growing of a crop in main field and possibility of growing more number of crops in main field increases. It is highly suitable for small seeded crops like rice and ragi, which require shallow sowing and frequent irrigation.

Pre-monsoon Sowing

In pre monsoon sowing, sowing is taken up in dry soil with summer rains, generally week before the anticipated receipt of monsoon rains. The seeds will germinate after the receipt of the rainfall. It is known as dry sowing or pre-monsoon sowing, the entire rainfall received is efficiently utilized in this sowing method.

Crop Geometry

The arrangement of plants in different rows and columns in an area to efficiently utilize the natural resources is called crop geometry. Crop geometry can be altered by changing the inter or intra row spacing. It is otherwise the area occupied by a single plant. The spacing for hybrid Napier grass is 50 cm x 50 cm, which means a single plant is occupying the area of 2500 sq. cm (0.25 sq.mt). Crop geometry is very essential to utilize the resources like light, water, nutrient and space optimally. Different crop geometries are available for fodder crop production.

Random Crop Geometry

In random crop geometry, spacing is random and it is in sowing methods like broadcasting. The risk of the same is exploitation or underutilization of natural resources.

Square Plant Geometry

Plants which require no restriction on all directions are given square planting. The plants are sown at equal distance on either side. Mostly perennial crops are cultivated under square planting geometry in which R to R = C to C. The advantages are uniform light availability, free and smooth movement of wind and possibility for mechanization.

Rectangular Method of Sowing

There are rows and columns, the row spacing are wider than the spacing between plants. This method facilitates easy inter cultivation and irrigation and mainly practiced for annual crops.

Types in rectangular Method

a) Solid row

Each row will have no proper spacing between the plants. This is followed only for annual crops which have tillering pattern. There is definite row arrangement but no column arrangement, e.g., Desmanthus.

b) Paired row planting

It is also a rectangular arrangement. It a crop requires 60 cm x 30cm spacing and if paired row is to be adopted the spacing is altered to 90 cm instead of 60 cm in order to accommodate an intercrop. The base population is kept constant. The space available between the rows can be used for intercrop planting.

c) Skip row

A row of planting is skipped and hence there is a reduction in population. This reduction is compensated by planting an intercrop and it is mostly practiced in rainfed or dryland agriculture.

Triangular Method of Planting

This method is practiced for trees and long duration crops. In this method, the number of plants per unit area will be more.

Importance of Crop Geometry

Firstly, crop geometry decides the crop population in a given area, thus crop geometry affects the crop growth and yield as well. High plant population may deplete soil moisture especially under rainfed conditions and low plant population will not utilize the soil moisture adequately. When soil moisture and nutrients are at optimum, reasonable high plant population is essential to utilize the natural resources like soil moisture, nutrients and sun light to ensure high production and productivity. Optimum plant population is a point above which increase in plant population will decrease the yield. Considering that maximum yield is mostly coincide with optimum plant population and fixing a optimum plant population for every fodder crop is a part of good agricultural practices.

Seed Germination

Germination is the basic life process in which the sown plant seeds are grown into young plants or seedlings. Based on their growing conditions and the fate of the cotyledons, the process of germination is classified into two main types:

1. Epigeal Germination
2. Hypogeal Germination

Hypogeal Germination

In this kind of germination, the cotyledons do not come out of the soil surface. In such seeds the epicotyl (i.e., part of embryonic axis between plumule and cotyledons) elongates pushing the plumule out of the soil. All monocotyledons show hypogeal germination. Among dicotyledons, gram, pea, groundnut are some common examples of hypogeal germination.

In monocotyledons (e.g., wheat, maize, rice, coconut) radicle and plumule come out by piercing the coleorrhiza and coleoptile respectively. The plumule grows upward and the first leaf comes out of the coleoptile. The radicle forms the primary root which is soon replaced by many fibrous roots.

Epigeal Germination

In seeds with epigeal germination, the cotyledons are brought above the soil due to elongation of the hypocotyl. In castor, cotton, papaya, onion, flat green leaf like cotyledons can be seen in the young seedlings. Here the cotyledons, besides food storage, also perform photosynthesis till the seedling becomes independent. In some other plants like bean, the cotyledons being thick, do not become leaf-like they shrivel and fall off after their food reserves are consumed by the seedling.

Special Germination

Vivipary (Viviparous Germination)

Vivipary is the phenomenon of giving birth to young ones in advanced stage of development. It occurs in mammals (among animals) and mangrove plants.

In mangrove plants (e.g., Rhizophora, Sonneratia, Heritiera) the seeds cannot germinate on the ground because of the excessive salt content and lack of oxygen in marshy habitat. In such plants seed dormancy is absent.

The embryo of the seed (present inside the fruit) continues growth while the latter is attached to the parent plant. Hypocotyl elongates and pushes the radicle out of the seed and the fruit. Growth continues till the hypocotyl and radicle become several centimetres long (more than 70 cm in Rhizophora). The seedling becomes heavy.

As a result it breaks its connection with the fruit and falls down in the salt rich muddy water in such a position that the plumule remains outside the saltish water while the tip of the radicle gets fixed in the mud. This protects the plumule. The radicle quickly forms new roots and establishes the seeding as a new plant.

Irrigation

Irrigation in agriculture is a time immemorial practice and probably it would have been the foundation for all agrarian civilization developed in river banks throughout the world. The development of scientific irrigation had humble beginning and Kallanai (The Grand Anaicut) constructed in early Chola period (300 BC) across the river Cauvery of Tamil Nadu state is an classical example for the importance irrigation in agriculture and water management in the ancient period. Early Mauryan King Samudragupta and Ashoka also took great interest in the construction of wells and tanks for agriculture irrigation. Development of agriculture irrigation continued all through history including post independence period of India.

Irrigation is the art and science of applying water externally in addition to rainfall to have year round production in a crop in the same piece of land. Irrigation in other hand can be called as application of water to cope up with the evaporation and transpiration demand of the soil and plant and the plant has to maintain the turgid water potential in order to satisfy the transportation of all nutrients and minerals. The sources of water for irrigation are wells, canals, tanks, pond, tube wells etc.

Concepts in Soil Moisture

Water present in the soil is referred as the soil moisture and divided in to three categories viz., gravitational water, capillary water and hygroscopic water.

Gravitational Water

Water held between 0.0 to 0.33 bars (0 to -33 kpa) soil moisture tension, that moves downward freely under the influence of gravity to the water table is termed as gravitational water. It is also referred to as free water. Gravitational water is of no use to plants as it drains out due to gravity. It reduces aeration in the soil and hence, its removal from soil is necessary for optimum plant growth.

Capillary Water

Capillary water is the water held in the capillary pores (micro pores) of the soil. Capillary water is retained on the soil particles by surface forces, adhesion i.e., attraction of water molecules for soil particles, cohesion i.e., attraction between water molecules to surface tension. Adhesion is a process of the attraction of solid surface for water molecules and forms a very thin film of water at solid-liquid interface. On the other hand, cohesion is attraction for each other. Capillary water is held between tensions of about 0.33 bars to 31 bars for the availability of the crops.

Hygroscopic Water

It is the water held tightly to the surface of soil particles by adsorption forces. It is essentially non-liquid and moves primarily in the vapour form. This water is unavailable to the plants as huge pressure force would be needed to extract it.

Sources of Water

Rainfall is the ultimate source of all kind of water. Based on its sources of availability it can be classified as surface water and subsurface water. Surface water includes precipitation (including rainfall and dew) water available from rivers, canals, tanks, ponds lakes and all kinds of water bodies. Besides, snowfall could able to contribute some quantity of water in heavy snowfall area like Jammu, Kashmir and Himalaya region. Subsurface water includes subsurface water contribution, underground water, well water etc.

Saturation Capacity

This is the maximum water holding capacity of the soil in which all the soil pores (Macropores and Micropores) are completely filled with water.

Field capacity (FC)

The soil moisture content after 2-3 days of irrigation and after drainage of gravitational water soil moisture content has become relatively stable. At the field capacity, the large pores are filled with air and the micro pores are filled with water. It is considered as the upper limit of water availability to plants.

Permanent Wilting Point (PWP)

It is the point of soil moisture at which plants can no longer obtain enough moisture to meet their requirement and remain wilted (not dead) unless water is added to the soil and considered as the lower limit of available water to the plant. If the water is not available further more plants will die.

Wilting Coefficient

The percentage of moisture in root zone of plant at the permanent wilting of plants is called wilting coefficient or critical moisture point.

Available Water

It is the moisture available for maximum plant use and arrived by subtracting the water at Field Capacity and water at the Permanent Wilting Point (PWP).

Ultimate Wilting Point (UWP)

The moisture content at which the wilting is complete, and the plants die is called Ultimate Wilting Point. At Ultimate Wilting Point, the soil moisture tension is as high as -60 bars

Crop Water Requirement

Water requirement of a crop is defined as the quantity of water needed for normal crop growth and yield in a period of time at a place and may be supplied by precipitation or by irrigation or by both.

Water is needed mainly to meet the demands of evaporation (E), transpiration (T) and metabolic needs of plants, all together known as consumptive use. In current situations, water is the scarce resource for crop production and considered as the most critical resource for future agriculture developments. Water use efficiency can be increased through introduction of suitable crop cultivars for minimum water usage, drought tolerant crop cultivars, devising optimum irrigation regime and methods, methods of reducing evaporative water loss from soil etc.

Approaches in Irrigation

The approaches of irrigation are classified in to three namely Soil moisture depletion approach, Climatological approach and Critical stage approach.

Soil Moisture Depletion Approach

When the soil moisture in a specified root zone depth is depleted to a particular level, it should be replenished by irrigation. In this approach, irrigation is scheduled based on the level of soil moisture depletion for a particular at a particular time.

Climatological Approach

In this approach, evapotranspiration of a plant is taken as indicator for scheduling the irrigation. Combination of soil moisture depletion and climatological can also be used irrigation scheduling.

Critical Stage Approach

In this method irrigation is based on critical moisture sensitive period, which means a point of lack of moisture led stress leads to irrevocable damage to growth and yield of a crop and irrigation at this stage is compulsory.

Methods of Irrigation

Broadly, irrigation methods are classified in four namely Surface irrigation, Sub surface irrigation, Over head or sprinkler irrigation and Drip irrigation.

Surface Irrigation

In surface irrigation systems, water is allowed to move across the surface (furrow or basin) of agricultural lands, in order to wet and infiltration of water into the soil and it is the most common method of irrigation and often called as flood irrigation. Surface irrigation can be classified in three namely furrow irrigation, basin irrigation, (check basin irrigation and ring basin irrigation) and border irrigation.

In furrow irrigation, small channels called furrows are formed and that will carry down the water as per the slope of the land. The crop is usually grown on the ridges between the furrows and it is suitable for all row crops. In basin irrigation, flat areas of land surrounded by low bunds are formed called as basin, and water will be filled in this basin for irrigation mostly used for tree farming. There are two types of basins namely check basin (forming small plots for water filling) and ring basin (circular basins) for water filling and both are in usual practice.

In border Irrigation water can be fed to the border of the land by a channel opening or water pipe opening and a sheet of water will be allow to flow down as per the slope of the land guided by the ridge bunds on either side.

Sub Surface Irrigation

In sub surface irrigation instead of wetting the surface of the soil, water is fed directly to the soil through capillary there by easing the water intake of crops. It uses pipes or tubes or drip tape buried in the soil to provide the water needs of the crops or plants. The advantages are prevents the loss from evaporation and improves crop yields by minimizing the incidences of disease and weeds. In this irrigation though the surface soil is dry, the root zone will be wet.

Sprinkler Irrigation

In sprinkler or overhead irrigation is process of distributing water through overhead high pressure sprinklers or rain guns. If it is permanent setup it is called as solid set irrigation system and moving sprinkling systems are also available for small farms. In this sprinkler system of irrigation, water is sprayed with pressure on the top of crop and soil in the form of a thin spray similar to rain fall. This system consists of pumping unit, main water lines, risers and nozzles for water spray with water flow regulatory control. This system is suitable for all the fodders crops and pasture management and especially for slope lands. It is water efficient up to 40-50 per cent and labour saving also.

Drip Irrigation

Drip irrigation is the latest method of irrigation has the origin of Israel and it is the most water efficient method. In this system water is delivered drop by drop near the root zone of the crop through pipe lines and it is also called as trickle irrigation. Water efficiency of this system is up to 80 per cent and it is best method of irrigation all the plantation crops, tree crops and fodder crops and highly suitable for water scare areas.

Drainage in Agricultural Lands

The removal of excess water from the surface of agricultural lands or from the root area of the crop is called drainage. Rainfall is the most common source of excess water apart from other sources of water for irrigation. The excess water load from rainfall is not only depends on the amount of rainfall but also on the storage capacity of the soil and on the rate of evapotranspiration. Part of the rainfall may be stored effectively in the soil for the use of plants or be readily evaporated, and the remaining excess water needs to be removed from the land.

Types of Drainage Systems

Two most commonly used techniques in drainage of agricultural fields are surface and subsurface drainage systems.

Surface Drainage

Surface drainage is the removal of excess water from the soil surface to prevent damage of crops from excess water. Surface drainage is a suitable technique where excess water from rainfall or surface irrigation cannot infiltrate into the soil and move through the soil to a drain, or cannot move freely over the soil surface to a natural / artificial drainage channel. Surface drainage problems mostly occur in flat or nearly flat areas, having uneven land surfaces preventing natural runoff through outlet.

Types of Surface Drainage

Random Field Ditch Method

Standing water may be present in the field at several places distributed randomly. These depressions or micro ponds are connected by means of shallow channels or ditches and these are led into an common outlet.

Land Smoothing

Land smoothing is a process of cutting of excess soil in elevated place and spread over lower areas, so that the surface will be even with uniform slope. Excess surface run off is collected and conveyed into the field ditches provided at the lower end of the field.

Bedding

Small furrows are formed at known intervals parallel to the slope for draining out water and known as dead furrows. The land between these furrows is known as beds. Small ridge or bund is made at the centre of the bed with gradual slope to drain water into the dead furrows.

Broad Bed and Furrow Method

The field is laid out into 90 cm beds and 45 cm wide furrows across the slope. About 0.5 per cent slope is provided for the furrows for free drainage. Crops are sown on the beds and furrows help in drainage of water when there is excess water.

Subsurface Drainage

Subsurface drainage is a process of removal of excess soil water to prevent damage to crops because of a high water table. Subsurface drainage problems occur in the shallow water table areas (areas near by water bodies) and the reasonable factors are substantial groundwater recharge and sluggish subsurface outflow.

Subsurface field drains can be either open ditches or pipe drains. Pipe drains are installed underground at depths normally ranging from 1 to 3 meters. Excess groundwater enters the perforated field drains and flows by gravity to an open or closed drain. When surface drainage is not possible due to subsoil conditions, water table and topography, subsurface drainage is resorted to remove ground water, or to lower water table. Unlike open drainage, land is not wasted and there is no interference to farming operations by subsurface drainage. However, this requires high investment cost for effective functioning.

Benefits of Drainage System

The purpose of drainage in agricultural fields are providing optimum soil water to the crop and maintaining well drained soil conditions for optimum growth of the crop. Good draining will offer better air movement in the soil and root respiration. It will also offer improved growth of beneficial soil bacteria which in turn enhances the availability of soil organic matter and nutrients to crops.

Drainage will alter physical properties of the soil and improve the infiltration capacity of soil and reduces the soil erosion. It maintains the proper soil temperature and accelerates the growth of plants. Good draining will improve the leaching of soil and prevents the salinity of the soil. The other benefits of the drainage are establishment good root system with larger coverage of soil for nutrient extraction, improved water holding capacity, less run off and cost effective labour utilization in tillage operations.

Weed Management

Weed is a complex term to understand. In agriculture, it is a plant which grows, where it is not wanted or not desired. But at the same time, it may have a other use in other place. Identification of a weed in particular situation is very subjective in nature. It does not identify a particular portion of plant kingdom but it depends upon the situation, in which the vegetation occurs. Bermuda grass – (*Cynodon dactylon),* Anjan grass – (*Cenchrus ciliaris), Rhodes grass (Chloris gayana*) are excellent pasture grasses but troubleshooting weeds in crop fields.

Based on the assessment of production losses due weeds, it forms the single largest factor causing losses in agriculture production more than pests and diseases to the tune of 40 per cent. Considering that, weed management is becoming a subject of interest in agronomy.

Characteristics of Weeds

As the weed plants are nourished by nature they bear more tolerant to adverse conditions in a particular situation, compared to domesticated crop

plants. However, the special characteristics of weeds are perpetuation, multiplication, dissemination, stabilization and overall adaptation.

Difficulty in Weed Control

1) Weeds are prolific with abundant seed production potentialities
2) They are comparatively resistance to control.
3) Long periods of dormancy and possessing deep root system
4) They can also reproduce by vegetative method.
5) Weeds have smaller seeds which help in easy dispersal

Methods of Weed control

- Good Husbandry Practices in crop production
- Physical destruction methods
- Herbicidal management methods
- Biological control methods

Integrated Weed Management

Integrated weed management is method where by all economically, ecologically and toxicologically justifiable methods are employed to keep undesirable plants or weeds below the threshold level of economic damage. It also includes a weed management program with a combination of preventive, cultural, mechanical, and chemical practices.

Principles of Integrated Weed Management

1) Manipulation of main crop habitat by utilizing some biological difference between the crops and weeds so as to place the crops in competitive advantage over weeds.
2) Taking measures to reduce the survival mechanism of weeds in soil.
3) Good crop husbandry practices should be followed, which will avoid the establishment of perennial and parasitic weeds
4) Keeping the weed management eco friendly

5) Flexibility in weed management program to try possible innovations based on the experiences.

Good Husbandry Practices in crop production

Good Husbandry Practices in crop production is the first step in effective management and there is no good substitute to good crop husbandry methods in crop lands and these are referred as ecological management methods in weed management. It includes, selective of crop, stale seed beds, crop rotations, summer fallowing, competitive cropping and selection of right season for planting crops etc.

Physical Control of Weeds

Physical or non chemical or mechanical methods of weed control utilize manual energy, animal power, or implements that dig out and remove the weeds. The implements used for physical control of weeds vary from simple hand tools to complex, multi tined weeding machines run by tractors. Manual weed control is a labour intensive method. Limitations are the presence of too wet or too dry soil condition at the time of weeding.

Herbicidal Control of Weeds

Herbicides are chemicals capable of killing or inhibiting the unwanted growth of plants and vegetation. There are number of herbicides available in the market and they vary in their molecular structures, mobility within plants selectivity, fate of herbicide in soils etc. In chemical methods, resistance will be a problem in long term use.

Advantages of Herbicide Method

1. Herbicide will be a choice, when seasonal limitation like rains blocking the use of manual or mechanical weeding program.
2. Herbicides may eliminate the crop weed interference even at very early stage of crop growth.
3. Herbicide can kill many weeds that survive by mimicry.
4. Herbicidal control does not dictate strict crop row spacing as warranted for mechanical or manual methods.
5. Herbicide brings about longer lasting control of perennial weeds by translocating in to deeper underground parts of weeds.
6. Herbicides are convenient to use on spiny and objectionable weeds

7. Herbicides spray reach easily the weeds growing in obstructed situations like under trees.
8. Herbicide usages reduce labour problem, greater possibility of farm mechanization, easier crop harvesting and lower cost of farm operations.

But at the same time, selection of right herbicide, time, method and rate of application skills are prerequisites for farmers. Crop selection and intercropping with various crops are restricted. Herbicides drift wash-off and runoff can cause considerable damage to neighboring crops.

Biological Control of Weeds

The biological control of weeds involves the use of living organisms such as insects, fish, other animals, disease causing organisms and competitive plants to limit weed infestations. Biological weed control is the use of living organisms to lower the population level or competitive ability of a weed species so that it is no longer an economic problem. Mode of action of biological methods of weed control is as follows,

1. It does not necessarily kill the weeds but it causes restricted in competitive or reproducing ability of the weeds
2. Slow in action and result, comparatively expensive than other methods.
3. Biological control is more effective in mono weed situations.
4. Eco friendly
5. Biological weed control is often permanent but it does not completely eradicate the weed.

Harvesting

Harvesting in agriculture is collecting the useful and economic value part or parts of a plant and it is carried out when all those parts have reached the desirable degree of maturity. Harvested product may be a grain, leaf, fruit, root or any other part of the plant, which depend on the nature of plant and its product. Time and method of harvest influences the quality and quantity of yield of a agricultural product. Generally the crops are harvested when it matures. It means, the crops are harvested at physiological maturity, harvest maturity and at storage maturity depends on the situation or need of produce.

Physiological Maturity

The crop said to be at physiological maturity, when the translocation of photosynthates (sugar like substances produced by photosynthesis) is stopped to the economic part. It is refers to the developmental stage, after which, there is no dry matter increase in the economic product. In cereals, the moisture content of grains is high during milky stage and gradually decreases due the accumulation of photosynthates. Physiological maturity indicated by a sudden fall in moisture content from 40 per cent to 20 per cent. At this stage, translocation of carbohydrates is stopped due to formation of abscission layer between rachis to grain. At this stage, the plant attains maximum dry weight; addition of inputs at this stage will not have any yield benefit. If the grains are harvested before this stage, it would have low dry matter and poor quality.

Harvest Maturity

Harvest maturity time a period in which product of interest of a plant is at its best quality and maximum yield. In certain grains, the crops are harvested at 25 per cent moisture content but most of the grain crops are harvested at 15-18 per cent moisture content. When the crop is grown for forage, the best time of harvest is when the crop attained maximum vegetative yield coupled with high quality. It is good to harvest at the time of ear head emergence stage for fodder. Harvest maturity generally occurs at 7 to 10 days after physiological maturity. Symptoms of harvesting are yellowing of leaves, drying of pods etc. The crop is harvested at physiological maturity only to vacate the field for next sowing of crops otherwise all the crops are harvested at harvest maturity.

Storage Maturity

When there is no scope for post harvest drying, the crops is to be harvested at the stage when it can be directly stored. The desirable moisture content for grain is less than 14 per cent. The other factors to be considered for harvesting the fodder are purpose of harvest like stall feeding, preservation, change in nutritive value, presence of toxins if any etc. As the age increases fibre content of the fodder will also increase and relatively protein content will decrease. In some of the crops like sorghum, toxins will be a prohibitive factor on harvest. Harvesting may be delayed for more dry matter accumulation when it is used for hay making and for stall feeding, early harvest is preferred for succulent fodders.

Methods of Harvesting

Manual Harvesting

Manual harvesting is a common method in small scale and developed countries farming system. Sickle, spade, digging rods and knifes are used as traditional tools for harvesting and digging and it is labour intensive. For indeterminate crops like pulses periodical picking of pods has to be done at the interval of 15 days.

Mechanized Harvesting

The reapers are used for harvesting and they are tractor side mounted, tractor front mounted, power tiller operated, self propelled walking and self propelled riding are being used for harvesting wheat, rice, finger millet etc especially in large scale farming systems.

Combined Harvesting

Combined harvester is used for rice, wheat etc, will efficiently utilize the labour especially for large scale paddy and wheat farming in developing.

Threshing Equipment

Animal drawn thresher are used now replaced with power thresher, multi-crop threshers are ideal for cereals, pulses and oilseed crops.

Problems in Harvesting

When the harvest coincides with heavy rain and cyclones, there will be a problem in harvesting the crop at maturity. The crops may be submerged and the seed will starts germinating on the plant itself. When the economic part is underground, harvesting is difficult if the soil dries due to lack of moisture.

Activity

1. Calculate the germination per cent of various crops sown in your farm
2. Collect the data on the efficiency of different tillage implements of your farm
3. Do the treatment for various seeds of your farm
4. Discuss the advantages and disadvantages of micro irrigation system

Exam Corner

1. What is agronomy?
2. What is tillage?
3. Difference between primary and secondary tillage
4. What is seed rate?
5. What is seed treatment?
6. List the methods of sowing
7. List the types of soil moisture
8. What is PWP and UWP in soil moisture?

9. What is drainage in agriculture?
10. What is plant protection?
11. What is weeding in agriculture?
12. What is harvest in agriculture?

5

Manures and Fertilizers

Learning Objectives

- Discuss the functions of manures and fertilizers
- Explain the use of various organic manure
- Explain the concept of compost and vermicomposting
- Explain the various chemical fertilizers available in market

Plants requires a number of nutrients for their growth and reproduction, of which six are primary in nature and they are,

1. Carbon - Plants are taking carbon from the air and soil
2. Hydrogen from water
3. Oxygen from water and air
4. Nitrogen from soil and it helps plants to synthesize protein for their growth they need to produce new tissues. Nitrogen is often in shortage in soil for the plants, and plants will try to take as much available from the soil at the same time too much of nitrogen will help the foliage growth and but not the setting of flowers and fruits.
5. Phosphorus stimulates root growth and helps the plants set flowers and seeds. Organic matter and activity of soil organisms increases the availability of phosphorus.
6. Potassium supports the overall vigor of the plant. It helps the plants make carbohydrates and provides disease resistance. It also helps in regulating the metabolic activities of the plant

Three secondary nutrients required comparatively in small quantities for the plant growth are Calcium, Magnesium and Sulphur. Calcium is primarily used by plants in cell membranes, at their growing points, calcium improves soil structure and helps bind organic and inorganic particles together.

Magnesium is the only metallic component of chlorophyll. Without it, plants can't process sunlight. Sulfur is a component of many plant proteins.

Micronutrients required by plants are boron, copper, iron, molybdenum, zinc, chlorine and manganese. Apart from natural sources like air, water and soil, manures and fertilizers are the sources for nutrients for the plant growth.

Manures and Fertilizers

The manures are organic products made of plant or animal origin; contain organic matter in large proportion and plant nutrients in small quantities used to improve soil fertility and productivity by modifying the soil physical, chemical and biological properties. Manures can also called organic fertilizers because of its richness in organic matter. Manures contribute to the fertility of the soil by adding organic matter and nutrients, such as nitrogen, that are trapped by bacteria in the soil.

On the other hand, fertilizer is any dry or liquid material added to the soil in order to supply one or more plant nutrients and term fertilizer is generally applied to commercially manufactured materials with some exceptions like lime and gypsum

Comparison of Manures and Fertilizers

Sl.No.	Manures	Fertilizers
1	Contain good amount of organic material there by improves the physical properties of the soil	Do not contain organic matter, will not alter the physical properties of the soil
2	Improves soil fertility as well as productivity	Improves soil fertility and productivity will not be improved always
3	Minimal concentration of all plant nutrients	Higher concentration of one or more plant nutrients
4	Bulky	Not Bulky
5	Nutrient availability will be slow based on the decomposition	Nutrients readily available
6	Long term effects	Short term effects
7	No salt effect	High salt effect
8	No adverse effect	Adverse effect in overdosing and in improper time

Organic Manure

Organic Manure can be classified in to two namely, bulky organic manure (Farm Yard Manure) and concentrated organic manure (oil cakes of plant origin). Bulky organic manure is of two types namely decomposed animal and plant waste cum residues (Composts of animal origin like cow, sheep, goat, poultry manure) and green manure (plants rich in nitrogen). The examples of the concentrated organic manure are mustard oil cake, neem oil cakes, groundnut oil cakes etc. The examples of green manure are undecomposed plants of Dhaincha, Sunhemp, Glyricidia and other leguminous crops.

Bulky organic manures include farm yard manure (FYM), farm compost, town compost, green manures and other bulky sources of organic matter. These manures are bulky in nature and supply plant nutrients in small quantities and organic matter in large quantities of which farm yard manure and green manure are important and most widely used for fodder production.

Functions of Bulky Organic Manures

1. Increase the organic matter content of the soil and thereby increase the humus content of soil and water holding capacity of sandy soil and improving the drainage of clay soil.
2. It act as a substrate for soil microorganisms thereby increase activity of microbes which in make the plant nutrients into available forms.

Farm Yard Manure (FYM)

Farm Yard Manure is the decomposed mixture of dung and urine of farm animals along with litter and the residual material from roughages or fodder fed to the cattle. On an average well decomposed Farm Yard Manure contains 0.5 per cent nitrogen 0.2 percent phosphorous and 0.5 per cent potassium. FYM is one of the most important agricultural by products in especially in our traditional farming and organic farming systems. Poultry manure is one of the richest organic manure contains 1.46, 1.17 and 0.62 per cent NPK.

The factors affecting the nutritional content of farm yard manure are age of the animal, feed quality, types of litters, ageing of manure and storage conditions. Farm yard manure consist of two portions namely dung and urine, in which half of the nitrogen and potassium present in the dung and phosphorous primarily present in the dung, considering that both and dung and urine will be stored properly for better quality farm yard manure. Loss of nitrogen from the urine of cattle is mainly through gaseous loss of ammonia from animal sheds. Loss of ammonia from dung is through leaching in rainy seasons and volatilization from manure heaps stored in animal sheds and agricultural fields.

The promising methods for improved handling of farm yard manure are using trench for composting, Gobor gas plant method and effective field management of farm yard manure. Gobor gas manure is comparatively rich in nutrients than regular farm yard manure, apart it also offers fuel gas supply for cooking purposes. Avoiding long term heaping of farm yard manure in the field should avoided in proper field management of farm yard manure.

In general, application of farm yard manure to the tune of 10 tonnes will offer about 50, 20,50 kg NPK. But availability of these nutrients will not be immediate or in the year application. Except potash, one third nitrogen and two third of phosphate only will be available to plants on the year application and it is called as direct effect. The residual effect will be available to plant in subsequent years because of the slow acting nature of farm yard manure. Based on that, when the farm yard manure application is continuous on yearly basis, the crop yield will also increase due to the direct effect and residual effect of yester years and it is called cumulative effect.

Compost

Compost is composed of decomposed organic materials of plant and animal origin largely through aerobic decomposition. The composting procedure is simple and easy to practice by farmers and institutions in cities. Composting is largely a bio-chemical process in which microorganisms both aerobic and anaerobic decompose organic residue and lowers the Carbon Nitrogen ratio.

The end product of composting is well decomposed mixed organic matter known as compost. Generally, rural compost made of animal wastes, left over farm litters, weeds, straw, fallen leaves, husk, crop stubble, straw and wood ash etc. The factors affecting composting are availability of food materials to the micro organisms, moisture, aeration, temperature and reaction. There are two composting methods namely heap and pit composting, of which pit composting is comparatively superior considering the quality of the end product.

Vermicomposting

Vermicompost is the process of composting mixture of decomposing vegetable or food waste, bedding materials by using various species of worms in to a vermicast. The vermicast also called as worm castings, worm humus, worm manure and worm faeces is the end-product of the breakdown of organic matter by earthworms. These excreta have been shown to contain minimum contaminants and a higher nutrient density than the organic materials before vermicomposting.

The worms are generally *Eisenia foetida or Ensenia Andrei* (Red wigglers), white worms, and earthworms can also be used to create a heterogeneous Vermicompost. Vermicompost is a nutrient rich organic fertilizer and soil conditioner. Vermiculture means artificial rearing of worms and the scientific process of using them for the production compost. Earthworms eat cow dung or farm yard manure along with other farm wastes and pass it through their body and in the process convert it into Vermicompost. The town and urban non-toxic waste solid and liquid materials an also be converted into Vermicompost in the same manner. Earthworms not only convert garbage into valuable manure but keep the environment healthy.

Method of Preparation

Vermicomposting should be carried out in shaded place; an all sides open thatched roof shed in a mud floor with long axis in east west direction is an ideal place for composting. The length of shed can be increased depending upon the quantity of waste to be treated and desirable height is 6 feet and 8 feet at eave and ridge point. Elevated area is preferable for avoiding flooding in monsoon seasons.

A shed area of 15 feet X 12 feet is sufficient to construct three vermibeds of 12 feet X 3 feet with the spacing of 1 foot between the beds. This space is sufficient for the composting of 12 quintals of waste in a cycle of 40-45 days. The site marked for vermibeds on the raised ground is watered and a 4 to 6 inches layer of any slowly biodegradable agricultural residue such as dried leaves, straw, sugarcane trash etc. is laid over it after soaking with water. This is followed by spread of 1 inch layer of farm yard manure. Earthworms are released on each vermibed at the rate of 1 kg per quintal of cow dung and agri waste and 1.5 kg per quintal of household garbage non toxic waste.

Frequency of loading the waste is of two ways namely daily loading at the rate of 2 quintals per day per bed or bulk loading at the rate of 4 quintals per bed in cycle of 45 days. On the top of the loaded waste, a Jute mat is spread to protect the earth worms from brids and insects. Water has to be sprinkled as and when necessary to keep the bed moist. The waste is turned upside down fortnightly without disturbing the base layer of vermibed.

The appearance of black granular crumbly powder on the top of vermibeds indicates the harvest stage of the compost and watering should be stopped for atleast 5 days. The earthworms go down and the compost is collected from the top without disturbing the lower layers (vermibed). The first lot of Vermicompost is ready for harvesting after 2-2 ½ months and the subsequent lots can be harvested after every 6 weeks of loading. The vermibed is loaded for the next treatment cycle.

Culture of Earthworms

Prepare a mixture of cow dung and dried leaves in 1:1 proportion. Release earthworm at the rate 50 numbers per 10 kg mixture. and keep it in shade with enough moisture. Earthworms will multiply 300 times within one to two months. These earthworms can be used to prepare vermicompost.

Advantages of Vermicompost

Vermicompost is nutrient dense organic manure, free from most of the chemical contaminants and eco friendly. It will improve the soil texture, tilth aeration, water holding capacity, enhancing nutrient absorption and prevents the soil compaction. The average NPK value of quality vermicompost will be around 1.6, 0.7 and 0.8 per cent.

Biogas Production

Biogas is produced from the anaerobic digestion of organic waste like cattle dung, biomass from farm, kitchen, industrial waste, poultry dropping, night soil and municipal waste. Biogas is the mixture of gases primarily methane (CH_4), Carbon di-oxide (CO_2), Nitrogen and traces of Hydrogen Sulfide (H_2S).

Components of Biogas Plant

1. Mixing tank: The feed material is collected in the mixing tank. sufficient water is added and the material is thoroughly mixed into homogeneous mixture
2. Inlet pipe : The substrate is discharged into the digester through the inlet pipe
3. Digesters : The slurry is fermented inside the digester and biogas is produced through bacterial action
4. Gas holder or gas storage dome : The biogas gets collected in the gas holder, which holds the gas until the time of consumption
5. Outlet pipe: The digested slurry is discharged into the outlet tank through the outlet pipe
6. Gas pipeline: The gas pipeline carries the gas to the point of utilization viz., stove or lamp

Advantages of Biogas

- It is a self sustaining and eco-friendly fuel and produces nutrient rich slurry which can be used as manure for organic farming
- It prevents the health hazards of smoke in poorly ventilated rural households that use dung cake and fire-wood for cooking
- It helps in scientific disposal of animal wastes with value addtion

Concentrated Organic Manures

Concentrated organic manures contain higher percentages of major plant nutrients like N, P2O5 and K2O compared to bulky organic manures like FYM and compost. These concentrated manures are made from raw materials of animal or plant origin. The common concentrated organic manures are oil cakes, blood meal, fish manure, meat meal and wool waste. Oil cakes are of two types namely edible oil cakes and inedible oil cakes.

Edible oil cakes like coconut oil cake, ground nut oil cake, mustard oil cake are rich in protein; there by their demand in livestock feed preparation is high and not used as manure. However, spoiled oil cakes not fit for livestock feed can be used as manure. Inedible oil cakes like neem oil cake, mahua oil cake and castor oil cake can very well be used as fertilizer. Concentrated organic manure of animal origin like blood meal, bone meal, low quality fish meal and horn and hoof meal have good fertilizer value. Concentrated organic manures nutrients availability will be rapid (3-4 months) compared to bulk organic manures. Castor and neem oil cake are also having germicidal action apart from manurial value.

Green Crop Manuring

Green manure is a cover crop grown in the fields for specified period of time and ploughed under the soil for incorporation in to the soil, primarily to provide nutrients and organic matter to the soil there by improving the physical structure, nitrogen fixing capacity and fertility of the soil. It has multiple functions like offering nutrients and bio mass to the soil there by changing the physical structure of soil to improve the water holding capacity and aeration.

Two type of green manuring namely in situ green manuring and green leaf manuring. In situ green manuring refers the process of growing some crops in the actual agricultural field, ploughed after some time and buried in the soil itself. Generally, Sunhemp and Dhaincha are good examples for In situ green manuring. Green leaf manuring is adding green leaves of certain crop (Glyricidia, Leucanea and Dhaincha) of various places like bunds and wastelands in the agricultural fields to improve the soil fertility.

Chemical Fertilizer

Chemical fertilizer is defined as the chemical material having definite chemical composition with high analytical value and capable of supplying plant nutrients in available forms. They are concentrated, nutrient dense, readily available nutrient forms with high salt and low residual effect.

Considering the number of nutrient supplies, it may be classified in to three namely; complete fertilizer is a fertilizer which contains all three major nutrients namely Nitrogen, Phosphorous and Potash (NPK). Incomplete Fertilizers is a fertilizer which lacks any one of three major nutrients. The straight fertilizer is a one which suppliers only one primary nutrient. Mixed or Complex fertilizer is the fertilizer which contains more than one primary or major nutrient produced by the process of chemical reactions which will very often used in crops for labour efficiency.

Based on the nutrient supplies, fertilizers can be broadly divided in to three namely, nitrogenous, phosphatic and potassium fertilizers. The commonly used fertilizers for nitrogen, phosphorous and potash are Urea for nitrogen, Super Phosphate for phosphorous and Muriate of Potash for potassium in Indian farming conditions and they are all single or straight fertilizers. Since most of the Indian soils require nitrogen on continuous basis use of nitrogen fertilizer is very common in India.

Nitrogenous fertilizers can be classified in to four based on the chemical form of nitrogen, namely, Nitrate fertilizers (Sodium nitrate), Ammonical fertilizers (Ammonium Sulphate), Nitrate and Ammonical fertilizers (Ammonium Nitrate) and Amide fertilizers (Urea). Among the nitrogenous fertilizers, Urea is the mostly commonly used fertilizers because of its pro factors like good physical condition, high nitrogen content, cost effectiveness per unit of nitrogen etc.

Slow release fertilizers are the improved type in nitrogenous fertilizers in which nutrients are slowly released to ease the intake of nutrients by plants. Example for the same are pelletized (increase in granule size of fertilizer), chemically altered (Urea form) and Coated Urea (Neem oil or Sulphur coated urea) which comparatively costly than regular fertilizers, yet it is having promising advantages too in practical application.

Phosphatic fertilizers are classified in to three namely water soluble (Di Ammonimum Phosphate and Super Phosphate), Citric acid soluble (Di Calcium Phosphate and Bone Meal) and Water Insoluble (Rock Phosphate) of which Super Phosphate and Di Ammonimum Phosphate are commonly used fertilizers. Potasic fertilizers are broadly divided in to two namely fertilizer containing chlorine (Muriate of Potash) and other than chlorine (Sulphate of Potash and Potassium Nitrate), Muriate of Potash is a commonly used fertilizer.

Commercial complex fertilizers contain the all the primary nutrients in specific grades (NPK), homogenous, granular with good physical condition, application of the same will reduce labour cost using single fertilizer.

Fodder production is exclusive in livestock farms; farm managers of livestock farms should always focus on the use of organic manure like compost, vermi composting and green manuring rather than chemical fertilizers to reap the sustainable benefits of organic manures in terms of soil structure, activity and fertility. At the same time use of chemical fertilizer may not be avoided fully, there by judicious use of chemical fertilizers is recommended.

Nutrient composition of various chemical fertilizers				
Sl. No.	**Name of the fertilizer**	**Per cent**		
		Nitrogen N	**Phosphorous P_2O_5**	**Potassium K_2O**
Nitrogenous Fertilizers				
Nitrate fertilizers				
1	Sodium Nitrate	16	-	-
2	Calcium Nitrate	15	-	-
Ammonium fertilizers				
1	Ammonium Sulphate	20	-	-
2	Ammonium Chloride	24 to 26	-	-
Nitrate and Ammonium fertilizers				
1	Ammonium Nitrate	33 to 34	-	-
2	Calcium Ammonium Nitrate	20	-	-
3	Ammonium Sulphate Nitrate	26	-	-
Amide fertilizers				
1	Urea	46.2	-	-
Phosphatic Fertilizers				
1	Super Phosphate	-	16	-
2	Double Super Phosphate	-	32	-
3	Triple Super Phosphate	-	48	-
4	Di calcium Phosphate	-	35-38	-
5	Rock Phosphate	-	20-40	-
6	Raw Bone Meal	-	20-25	-
Potasic Fertilizers				
1	Muriate of Potash	-	-	60
2	Sulphate of Potash	-	-	48.5

Integrated Nutrient Management

Intensive agricultural production practices are focusing the wide spread use of chemical fertilizers and most of the situations it is also yielding results in productivity, long term results are not favorable in terms of soil structure, activity and fertility. At times over fertilization leads excess level of salts in soil leads to soil infertility and environmental pollution.

On the other hand, though the use of organic fertilizers offers incremental benefits, long term use offers sustainable benefits. But at the same time availability of organic manure is becoming limited and costly, prevents the sole use of the same for intensive agricultural production. Considering these situations, integrated use of organic and chemical fertilizer is becoming the order of the day for effective and efficient agriculture production including fodder production systems.

Integrated and judicious use of chemical fertilizers together with organic manures, farm wastes and bio fertilizers to improve the soil structure, activity and fertility for improved and sustainable agricultural productivity is called as Integrated Nutrient Management. The sources of nutrients for plants are soil, organic manures, mineral fertilizers and other bio fertilizers and the management of each source of nutrients will have a additive effect on the total fertility management of the soil.

Continuous use of soil for various crops in intensive agriculture will make the soil deficit in primary, secondary and micro nutrients, however soil erosion is also one of the critical factor for soil infertility, which can corrected only through good soil and moisture management and through the selection of ideal cropping program.

Careful collection, conservation and recycling of those organic wastes would enable India to meet its nutrient requirement and develop its agriculture on a sustainable and organic basis. Judicious use of chemical fertilizers at the right time in right place will avoid the negative effects of the same. Use of slow release chemical fertilizers also offer a scope for maximizes the benefits of the use chemical fertilizers. Use of bio fertilizers like Rhizobium, Azotobacter Azospirillum, Blue green algae inoculants can also be used to improve the productivity. Phosphatic biofertilizer like various soil bacteria and fungi of *Pseudomonas striata, Bacillus polymixa*, *Aspergillus awamori* posses the ability to bring insoluble phosphate in to soluble forms through secretion of organic acids and it is also potential role in integrated nutrient management system. Based on the above discussion, the combined use of organic, biological and inorganic fertilizers carves special significance as complementary and supplementary to each other in total soil fertility management.

Activity

1. Collect the data on the various organic fertilizers available around your farm area and offer your comments
2. Collect the data on the trade name, chemical composition and cost of various chemical fertilizers available in the market and offer your comments
3. Estimate the availability of various manures cow dung, sheep and goat droppings and poultry manure in your livestock farm and draw your inferences

Exam Corner

1. List the primary nutrients for plants
2. Difference between manure and fertilizer
3. What is organic manure?
4. What is farm yard manure?
5. What is NPK?
6. What is compost?
7. What is green manure and green leaf manure?
8. What is Vermicompost?
9. What is concentrated organic manure?
10. What is complete fertilizer?
11. What is straight fertilizer?
12. What is Integrated Nutrient Management?

6

Farm Machinery

Learning Objectives

- Discuss the role of farm machinery in agricultural operations
- List the farm machineries for various agricultural operations
- Discuss the primary and secondary tillage machineries

Farm machinery is a range of mechanical implements used in agriculture production from land preparation to harvesting and processing the produce. It includes various ploughs, tractors, broadcaster, harvester and post harvest processing machineries. The purpose of using machines in agriculture production is to handle the mass production, improve the efficiency and to save the labour costs. The types of implements used in fodder production are tillage, sowing, intercultural, plant protection and harvesting equipments.

Primary Tillage Implements

Country Plough

Country plough is the indigenous type plough made of wood with iron share. The parts of the plough are body, shoe, share, beam and handle. The share makes an angle of 10^0 to 30^0 with the ground level. It cut and opens the soil in V shape furrow and it will not invert the soil. The size and shape of country plough will vary depending on the regions of the country.

Mould Board Plough

It is one of the oldest and most important heavy tillage implement. It is imported to India during the British rule. To suit different soil conditions and crop requirements, mould board has been designed in different shapes. A mould board plough consists of a share, mould board, land side, frog and tail piece. It will cut open the soil, lift it and reverse the soil.

Disc Plough

It is one of the implement which can work in all types of soil specifically in hard and dry land. The discs on a plough are mounted on bearings. Disc depth of cut 1/3rd of disc diameter and disc width of cut is 0.4 times the disc diameter. Plough inverts the soil pan. Plough can be used for deep ploughing and it cannot be used at high speed because for cutting action for which slow speed is necessary. The parts of disc plough are hitch bolt, disc scraper, disc, disc hub, rear furrow wheel, beam or frame, lift crank and standard.

Chisel Plough

Chisel plough, is a popular farming tool used for deep tillage. It works to a depth of 45 cm at the maximum. Its main purpose is to loosen and aerate the soil while leaving crop residue at the surface of the soil. It reduces soil erosion, improves permeability of air and prevents sub soil crust formation.

Secondary Tillage Implements

Cultivator

It is a secondary tillage implement which breaks the clods formed and make the soil to fine tilth. It also control weeds and it also helps in loosening the soil after the crop establishment. It is used to mix the manure in the soil before sowing of crop. It is machinery with short narrow slightly curved shovels. Cultivator consists of 9 or 11 tynes attached to a rectangular frame. The tynes are staggered in two rows one behind the other. Spacing in between the tynes is adjustable. The bottom of the tynes are fitted with shovels, which are replaceable and reversible. The cultivator has two heavy coiled springs fitted with each tyne. The spring loaded tynes deflect when the tynes hit obstacles in the field with stones and root stumps. The operation capacity is 0.40 hectare per hour.

Rotovator

Rotovator or rotary tiller is a versatile tillage implement that uses a series of blades to crush and mix the soil before planting and also helps in removal of weeds. It provides better soil pulverization than other tillage equipment and it will Loosen and aerate the soil up to 10 to 15 cm depth. It removes previous crop residue entirely. Cutting of soil is done of blades on the rotor shaft. The rotor shaft consist of cutting blades of C, J or L shape. The rotovator gave an impact over soil and throw the soil to upward as of the rotational speed and pulverize the soil by breaking the clods. The components of the rotovator are cardan shaft, rotor shaft, trailing board, depth control skid, gear box and blades.

Disc harrow

Harrow is a secondary tillage implement that cut the soil to a shallow depth for smoothening, pulverizing the soil and also cut the weeds and mix the material with the soil. Disc harrow consists of concave cutting blades mounted on a common shaft. A disc harrow mainly consists of disc, gang, gang bolt, gang central lever, arbor bolt, bearings, transport wheels, scraper and weight box.

Leveller

Traditionally farmers level their fields using animal drawn or tractor drawn levellers. These levellers are implements consisting of a blade acting as a small bucket for shifting the soil from higher to the low-lying positions. It is seen that even the best leveled fields using traditional land leveling practices are not precisely leveled and this leads to uneven distribution of irrigation water.

The advanced method to level or grade the field is to use laser-guided leveling equipment. Laser land leveling is leveling the field within certain degree of desired slope using a guided laser beam throughout the field.

Bund Former

It is used for making bunds or ridges by collecting the soil. Bunds are required to hold water in the soil, thereby conserve moisture and prevent run off. The size of the bund former is determined by measuring the maximum horizontal distance between the two rear ends of the forming boards. A bund former consists of forming board, beam and a handle.

Ridger

A ridger is an implement which cuts and turns the soil in two opposite directions which forms ridges. It is also known as furrower, double mould plough or ridging plough. Ridger is used to form ridges, for sowing row crop seeds and plants in well tilled soil. The ridger is also used for forming field furrows or channels, earthing up and similar other operations in grown up crops. The ridger generally has V-shaped or wedge-shaped share, fitted to the frog. The nose or the tip of the share penetrates into the soil and breaks the earth. The mould boards lift, invert and cast aside the soil, forming deep channels and ridges of the required size. A ridger consists of beam, clevis, frog, handle, mould boards, braces, share, and sliding shoe.

Seed Drill

Seed drill is a machine used for placing the seeds in a continuous stream in furrows at uniform rate and at controlled depth with an arrangement of covering the seeds with soil. Seed drill opens the furrow with specified row spacing and particular depth. It carries the seeds in the seed drum, which will be placed in the furrow and it covers the seed with soil. Both seeds and fertilizer are placed by seed cum fertilizer drills.

Weeder

The tool normally used to remove the weed is the hand hoe. But it imposes drudgery in operation to cover vast area. With invention of long handled weeder, it become easy to operate and cover larger in a short period. There are two types of manually operated weeder namely Star type weeder and Peg tooth weeder. These weeder can be used only in row spaced crop and not in the broadcasted field. They consist of blade which cut the weeds by push and pull operation. Star type weeder is used in loamy soil, Peg tooth weeder used in clayey or heavy soil.

Power Weeder

Power weeder is farm implement utilized for eliminating weeds, undesirable plants, and grass, stir and pulverize the soil Power weeders are successfully utilized in wide spacing crops, where the weed management. It may be fuel or battery operated.

Sprayers

Agricultural sprayers have components like spray nozzle, liquid tank, sprayer pump, pressure regulator, valves. This agriculture sprayers comes in various size, design and performance specifications. There are small sprayers to very large sprayers in size that helps to cover small area of land to extensive land. Sprayers are mainly used to apply fertilizer, herbicide and pesticides on the crop. It can be manual or mechanical. There are number of sprayers which are designed for different spraying applications like gardening, crops, trees, fruit, livestock needs, and weed control. Various types of sprayers suitable for small to large lands are as follows:

1) Knapsack Sprayer
2) Portable Power Sprayer
3) Knapsack Power Sprayer
4) Mist Dust Sprayer
5) Tree Sprayers
6) Bucket sprayer

7) Compression sprayer

8) Air craft sprayer

Chaff Cutter

A chaff cutter is a mechanical device for cutting forages, fodder, straw and hay of various crops into small pieces to feed the livestock. This helps in the animal's digestion and prevents animals from rejecting any part of their fodder. Currently chaff cutters are available from basic hand operated model to machine operated with various speed, cutting capacity, length of chaffed fodders based on the preference of number of animals to be fed and class of livestock. The chaffed fodder are easy to transport, feed and digest by the animals. The main advantage of chaffing is avoiding selective intake of leaf, soft stems alone by the animals.

The main components of chaff cutter are feed hopper or trough, feed roller, fly wheel, cutting blades, shear plate etc. Based on the design it may be fly wheel type or cylinder type. Ideal chaffed fodder pieces length may be 25 mm to 40 mm for all classes of livestock. Commercially in motor operated chaff cutters, 1-5 HP motor powered chaffers are also available for our use depending of the quantity of cut fodder requirement per day. Blower type or tractor mounted chaff cutters also available for large scale use. Since, chaffing fodder is machine operated mechanical process, trained manpower, sufficient space for operation and careful maintenance are necessary to ensure safety.

Baler

Baler is the tractor drawn attachment used to make hay or straw from crop surplus. It is used to compress a cut or raked crop into compact bundle which is easy for transport and storing. Balers are divided into stationary balers, movable and field balers. They are further classified into square balers, rectangular balers and round balers according to the bale shape produced. According to density of bale, they could be high (200-350 kg/m^3), medium (100-200 kg/m^3) or low density (<100 kg/m^3) balers.

Activity

1) Draw the primary tillage implements
2) List the agricultural implements of your farm and describe their functions
3) Operate the sprayers and offer your comments
4) Operate the chaff cutter and observe the function of the same

Farm Machineries		
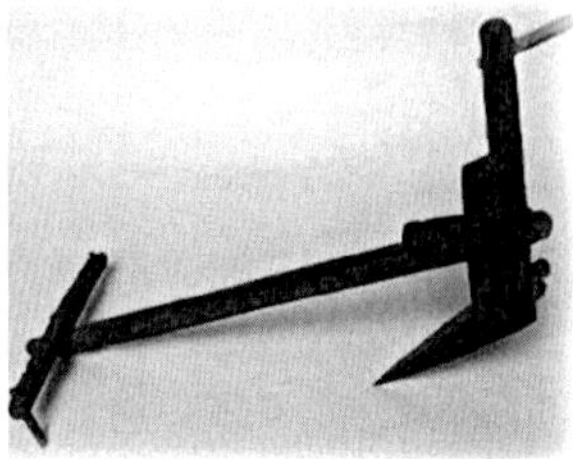		
Country Plough	Cultivator	Disc Plough
		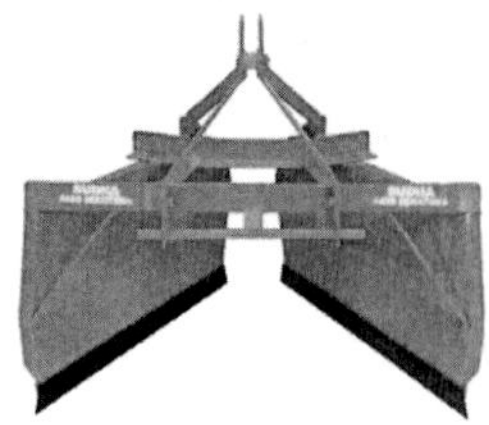
Mould Board Plough	Rotavator	Bund Former
		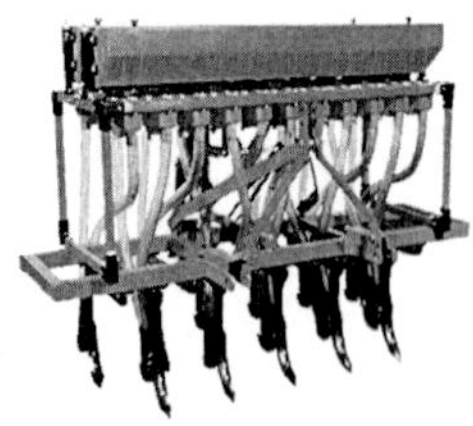
Ridger	Land Leveller	Seed Drill
	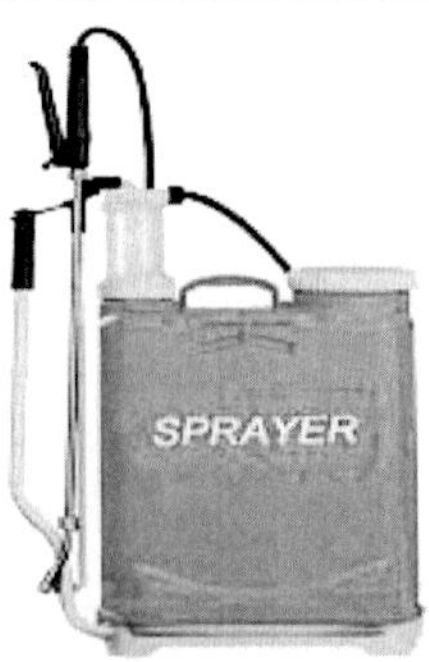	
Power Weeder	Sprayer for Agriculture	

Exam Corner

1. Define farm machinery
2. List primary tillage equipment
3. List second tillage equipment
4. What is cultivator?
5. What is rotavator?
6. What is disc harrow?
7. What is bund former?
8. What is ridger in farm machinery?
9. List the uses of sprayers?
10. What is chaff cutter?
11. What is leveler in field formation?
12. What is baler?

7

Introduction to Fodder Crops

Learning Objectives

- Explain the nature and function of fodder crops
- Discuss the classification of various fodder crops
- List the common cereal, grass and leguminous fodders
- Explain the package of practices of common fodder crops

In broad perspective, forages are plants and crops used for animal feeding. It includes all the natural and cultivated crops, shrubs, and trees etc., used in livestock feeding. Here, fodder specifically denotes the cultivated crops exclusively used for livestock feeding. Though, they are synonymously used in books, a student of veterinary science should able understand the difference between forages and fodder. Fodder is a term mainly used in intensive livestock farming where stall feeding is preferred over grazing to optimize the efficiency of production per unit area. Though, most of the tree's leaves are used for animal feeding, some of the trees being cultivated exclusively for animal feeding and those are called fodder trees and others called as multipurpose trees.

Classification of Fodder

In general, fodders can be classified in to three namely cereal, grass and leguminous fodders based on the botanical class. Here, cereal and grass are grouped in to non legumes because of their low protein levels and leguminous fodders will have high protein. Fodder Sorghum, Fodder Maize are examples of cereal fodders and Napier grass and Guinea grass are examples of grass fodder. Lucerne and Desmanthus are examples of leguminous fodders

Based on the duration of the crop, fodders can be classified in to two namely annual (within one year) and perennial (more than one year) fodders. Fodder Sorghum and Fodder Maize are come under annual fodders and Napier grass and Guinea grass comes under perennial fodders. Mostly, all the cereal fodders are come under annual fodders except the multi cut varieties of the same.

Based on the type of cultivation, fodders can be classified in to two namely irrigated fodder and rainfed fodders. Though all the fodders can be cultivated in rainfed condition, based on its duration of life cycle, annual cereal and legume fodders are generally cultivated in rainfed condition using rainfall as irrigation source. Perennial grass fodders and legumes are cultivated in irrigated condition to ensure round the year supply of green fodder to the farm. Multicult cereal fodder varieties area also cultivated in irrigated condition for the same purpose.

Based on the suitability of fodder for cut and carry system or pasture and grazing lands, fodders can be classified in to fodders suitable for intensive cultivation or suitable for pasture lands. Hybrid Napier and guinea grass, Lucerne and *Desmanthus*, are highly suitable for intensive cultivation and cut and carry system of rearing. *Cenchrus, Stylo* spp. are suitable for pasture and grazing lands. Height of the crop, resistance for grazing pressure and drought decides the suitability of the crop for a system of rearing.

Based on the suitability of crop with reference to climatic regions, fodders can be classified in to tropical and temperate fodders. Kikuyu grass, Lucerne and berseem are classical temperate fodders which can withstand cold and frosty conditions. On the other hand, Hybrid Napier, *Desmanthus* are examples of tropical fodders.

Fodder Based Feed Regimen

In Indian livestock farming scenario, fodder based feeding regimen of large and small ruminants are very popular, because of the reason that, grains, oil cakes, milling by products of cereals and pulses are scarce and costly. The popular cost effective feeding regimens for extensive, semi intensive and intensive livestock farming systems are fodder based only. The examples of fodder based feeding regimens are as follows

Extensive System of Rearing

Grazing is the main source of feeding with supplementary feeding in evening especially during lean seasons. It is the most cost effective feeding system and highly suitable for low input – low output farming systems

Semi Intensive System of Rearing

Grazing and feeding of additional cut fodder in stall feeding along with concentrate is the popular feeding method. It is suitable for medium input and output production system

Intensive System of Rearing

Stall feeding of cut fodder and concentrate feed is the popular method, it is highly suitable for high input – output production systems especially in urban areas. In intensive farming, fodder component may be grass plus concentrate, grass plus legumes plus concentrate depending on the availability of fodder. Where ever available hay or silage can be used.

Fodder Maize (*Zea mays*)	
Synonyms	English: Corn, Hindi: Makka, Telegu: Makka Jonne, Tamil: Makka Cholam Kannada: Makka Jola
Origin	Maize, commonly known as Corn is a cereal crop domesticated in Central and Southern Mexico. Maize crop was introduced to India during seventieth century by Portuguese. Fodder maize is a cereal fodder can be exclusively cultivated for animal feeding.
Description	Fodder maize is an annual crop. It is a tall, determinate, annual C4 plant with the height of one to four meters. It is producing large, narrow, opposing leaves, borne alternately along the length of a solid stem. Maize crop is mostly cross pollinated by wind and occasionally by insects. Male inflorescence is called as Tassel and female inflorescence is called as Cob.
Environment	Fodder maize can be grown in all seasons viz., Kharif, Rabi and Summer, when the irrigation is available. Fodder Maize cannot withstand drought or water logging condition. The desirable temperature is 18°C to 23°C and it grows well in drained and silty loam soils. The desirable soil pH range for fodder maize is 5 to 7. It can be grown up to 2500 meters MSL
Varieties	African tall, Ganga 5, Moti composite, Vijay composite, Jawahar, Pratap makka chari, J-1006, APFM 8
Field preparation	Two ploughings are essential. Land must be prepared to fine tilth condition and levelled for proper irrigation and drainage.
Manures and Fertilizer	Recommended farm yard manure is 12.5 tonnes per hectare at the time of second ploughing. Fertilizer can be applied as per soil fertility or otherwise as blanket recommendation of 60:40:20 kg NPK per hectare can be followed.
Seed rate and spacing	Seed rate is 40 kg per hectare and can sown with the spacing of 30 x 10 cm in ridges and furrows which helps in anchoring of proper roots
Irrigation	Life irrigation on third day of sowing, afterwards once in a week or as and when needed
Harvest	Harvesting at milk to early dough stage produces higher yield and protein content. Late dough stage is suitable for hay and silage. Desirable harvesting period is 60-70 days.
Biomass yield	The average biomass yield of maize is 40 tonnes per hectare. The mean DCP and TDN values are 6 per cent and 70 per cent on dry matter basis.
Intercropping	Maize can be intercropped with pulses like cowpea, soybean etc., with proper row arrangement. Under rainfed condition maize can be sown along with various millets and pulse crop.

Use in livestock feeding	Chaffed fodder maize can be used as green cereal fodder for dairy animals at the rate of 20-25 kg per animal per day. Chaffed fodder can be used for sheep and goats at the rate of 3-5 kg per animal per day. It is also a desirable cereal fodder for hay and silage.

Fodder Sorghum **(*Sorghum bicolor*)**	
Synonyms	English: Sorghum, Hindi: Jowar, Telegu: Jonna, Tamil: Cholam, Kannada: Jola, Malayalam: Cholam
Origin	Sorghum is a versatile crop of African origin, especially suitable for fodder cultivation in arid and semiarid tropical regions of India.
Description	Sorghum is a vigorous C4 grass may be annual or perennial in nature. The plant produce tillers, nodes and internodes are glabrous. It is a self pollinating crop. It can grow up to a height of 6-8 feet. The leaves are long and alternatively arranged. The strong stem is soft and juicy in nature and it is also called Camel crop because of its drought resistance.
Environment	Sorghum is a warm-weather crop, requires high air temperatures for good germination and growth. It grows wells in the temperature of 26-30 degree Centigrade. Loamy soil with high water retention capacity is suitable for fodder Sorghum cultivation. The crop is grown on soil with pH ranging from 5.5 to 8.5. It tolerates salinity and alkalinity to some extent.
Varieties	Annual sorghum varieties are Pusa Chari-1, Pusa Chari-6, MP Chari, UP Chari-1 , Co4, Co27,K7. Perennial sorghum varieties (multi cut varieties) are CoFS 29, CoFS 31, Pusa Chari-615.
Field preparation	Minimum of two ploughing are essential to obtain good tilth. Sorghum can be grown in beds and channel which can be formed with the help of bund former.
Manures and Fertilizer	Basal application of farm yard manure is 12.5 tonnes per hectare. In irrigated farming conditions, chemical fertilizer is applied at the rate of 30:40:20 kg NPK / ha in addition to basal application farm yard manure. In rainfed farming conditions recommended dose of chemical fertilizer is 30:20:0 kg NPK / ha in addition to basal application of farm yard manure. In perennial and multi cut fodder sorghum varieties cultivation 30 kg N has to be applied after every harvest.
Seed rate and spacing	In rainfed farming seed rate is 40 kg per hectare and in irrigated conditions it is 75 kg per hectare. The seed rate is 12.5 kg per hectare for perennial or multi cut sorghum varieties. Line sowing can be practiced in irrigated and rainfed conditions with the spacing of 30 x 10 cm. Rainfed crop has to sown by broadcasting on the onset of monsoon or as pre-monsoon sowing.
Irrigation	Irrigation required at once in a week or as and when necessary in irrigated farming conditions. In rainfed farming, 4-5 rainy days with the interval of 10 days is sufficient for good yield.
Harvest	The desirable time for harvest is 60 to 65 days after sowing or fifty per cent flowering stage in irrigated and rainfed farming for annual sorghum varieties. In multi cut varieties first harvest is at 65-70 days and subsequent harvests at the interval of 45-50 days.

Bio mass yield	Biomass yield in irrigated and rainfed farming conditions is 40 and 30 tonnes per hectare in annual varieties. The annual bio mass yield in multi cut fodder variety is 200 tonnes per hectare. The DCP and TDN content of fodder sorghum are 7 and 70 per cent.
Intercropping	In fodder sorghum, mixed cropping can also be practiced with fodder legumes, viz. cowpea, horse gram and cluster bean at the ratio of 2:1 to harvest cereal and legume fodders.
Use in live-stock feeding	Matured and chaffed sorghum fodder can be offered to dairy animals at the rate of 20-25 kg per day per animal and 3-5 kg per day per animal for sheep and goats. Sorghum is the most preferred fodder for hay and silage making in tropical areas.
Point of Ponder	Fodder sorghum is known for Hydrogen Cyanide (HCN) poisoning in ruminant feeding. High amount of HCN found in early growth stages and decreases as the crop attains maturity. Feeding of immature sorghum fodder should be strictly avoided to prevent the toxic effects of sorghum. Harvesting fodder at 50 per cent flowering stage is desirable for animal feeding.

Fodder Bajra (Pearl millet) (*Pennisetum glacum*)	
Synonyms	English: Pearl millet, Hindi: Bajra, Telegu: Sazzalu, Tamil: Cumbu, Kannada: Sajje, Malayalam: Cumbu
Origin	It is a small seed millet crop originated from West Africa
Description	Fodder bajra is a short duration C4 plant, drought resistant, quick growing and sweet stemmed plant. The leaves are alternate, linear and pubescent. It is an erect annual crop which produces more tiller.
Environment	It can be grown in areas where annual rainfalls range from 125 to 900 mm. Ideal growth temperatures range from 21 degree C to 35 degree C. Pearl millet is a crop that can grown in all types soil and known to tolerate acid sandy soils and also is able to grow on saline soils.
Varieties	Avika Bajra Chari (AVKB – 19), Gaint Bajra, CO-8, Baif Bajra-1, Narendra Chara Bajra-2, Gujarat Anand forage Bajra 4
Field preparation	Two ploughings are essential. Land must be prepared to fine tilth condition and levelled for proper irrigation and drainage.
Manures and Fertilizer	Recommended Farm Yard Manure is 12.5 tonnes per hectare at the time of second ploughing. Fertilizer can be applied as per soil fertility or otherwise as blanket recommendation of 50:40:20 kg NPK per hectare can be followed in addition to farm yard manure.
Seed rate and spacing	Fodder bajra requires a seed rate of 8-10 kg per hectare with the spacing of 30 X 10 cm. Line sowing or broadcasting can be followed.
Irrigation	Irrigation should be given once in 10 days or as and when necessary. In rainfed farming 4-5 rainy days with the interval of 10 days is sufficient.
Harvest and Biomass yield	The fodder crop can be harvested at 40-45 days after sowing and produce a yield of 40 tonnes per hectare
Intercropping	Fodder bajra can be intercropped with cowpea that can be harvested together to provide a nutritious fodder to livestock

Use in livestock feeding	Fodder bajra can be fed to the ruminants at all stages of its growth since it doesn't contain anti-nutritional factor, it contains about 12.5 per cent protein. Chaffed fodder bajra can be fed dairy animals at the rate of 20-25 per animal per day. The sheep and goats can be fed at the rate of 3-5 kg per animal per day.

Fodder Oats (***Avena sativa***)	
Synonyms	English: Oats
Origin	The origin of Oats is Asia Minor otherwise called Mediterranean Asia
Description	It is an annual crop grows to a height of 4-5 feet with fibrous root system. The clumps grow erect, smooth and hollow and leaves are linear and alternate.
Environment	Oats is a popular fodder crop of winter season and cold and dry climate is desirable for its cultivation. It grows at temperature of 15-25 degree C with the rainfall ranges of 80-100 mm. It can be cultivated in all kinds of soil except the alkaline or water logged soils.
Varieties	In general oats is meant for dual purpose of grain and fodder. Popular fodder varieties are Weston 11, Kent, OL 9,10,11, Brunker 10, HFO 114, OS 6, Bundle jai 851, UPO 94, UPO 50, OS 6, Algeria 19, UPO 212, OL-125, OL-265
Field preparation	Land should be ploughed twice to fine tilth and beds and channels are prepared for sowing
Manures and Fertilizer	Basal dressing application of Farm yard manure is at the rate of 10-12 tonnes per hectare. Basal dressing of 40 kg N and 40 kg P2O5 should be done at the time of seeding and 30 kg N should be applied as top dressing each after first and second cutting.
Seed rate and spacing	The desirable seed rate is 60 -70 kg per hectare for fodder production with line spacing of 20 -25 cm
Irrigation	Four irrigations at the interval of 10 days is sufficient in irrigated conditions and three rainy days with the interval 10 days is sufficient in rainfed farming
Harvest	The desirable harvest time for single cut oats is at milk stage and multi cut oats take first cut at 65-70 days after sowing and subsequent cuts at milk stage.
Bio mass yield	Biomass yield of fodder oats is 40-60 tonnes per hectare.
Use in livestock feeding	Chaffed oat fodder can be fed dairy animals at the rate of 20-25 kg per animal per day and for sheep and goats at the rate of 3-5 kg per day per animal. It is having DCP and TDN of 7.5 and 70 per cent.

Hybrid Bajra Napier Grass (***Pennisetum glacum* X *Pennisetum purpureum***)	
Synonyms	Hybrid Bajra Napier grass, Hybrid Napier Grass
Origin	It is an interspecific hybrid between bajra and Napier grass and combine qualities of faster growth of bajra with deep root system and multi cut habit of Napier grass.

Description	It is an erect, stout, deep rooted, perennial hybrid grass derived from inter specific cross between *Pennisetum glaucum* and *Pennisetum. purpureum*. The hybrid is a triploid and hence sterile. They are propagated by planting of two nodded stem cuttings or rootstocks. The leaves are large and green, the sheath is soft and the margins are less serrated. Among the grasses hybrid Napier Bajra is one of the popular grass fodder in terms of succulence, palatability, bio mass yield and nutritive value in livestock feeding. It is the most recommended grass fodder for cut and carry system of feeding.
Environment	The grass grows throughout the year in tropics and in a variety of soils. It grows well in deep, well drained loamy soil with a mean pH of 6-6.5 and the temperature between 25 and 40 degree C. It normally grows in areas with rainfall greater than 800 mm. It can tolerate moderate drought and susceptible to prolonged flooding. It can also be grown in shades of horticultural plantations like coconut gardens.
Varieties	DHN-6, Yashwant, NB 21, Co-4, IGFRI-7, BNH-10, APBN-1, IGFRI Hybrid Napier – 3,7,10, Pusa Giant, NB -21, Co-3, Co-4, Co-5, KKM 1, PBN-83, 233, 346
Field preparation	Since the hybrid Napier is perennial in nature with multi cut feature, the field should be prepared deep enough to withstand the crop for about 3-5 years. Deep plough with disc followed by cultivator and rotavator to obtain fine tilth.
Manures and Fertilizer	The recommended basal application of farm yard manure is 25 tonnes per hectare along with bio fertilizer like Azospirillum or Phosphobacteria at the rate of 2000 gram per hectare. Blanket recommendation for inorganic fertilizer is 150: 50 : 40 kg NPK per hectare in addition to the basal application of farm yard manure. Top dressing is 45 kg N on 30 days of initial planting. There after 30 kg N per hectare can be applied after every cut. Every year after 4th cut, apply 45: 40: 40 kg of NPK to sustain the fodder yield.
Seed rate and spacing	Hybrid Bajra Napier grass is vegetative propagated and the propagation material stem cuttings or root stocks. Considering the desirable spacing of 50 x 50 cm, the number of stem cuttings required is 40000 Nos per hectare
Irrigation	Hybrid Napier Bajra grass is highly suitable for irrigated farming only. Irrigation at the time of planting, three days after planting and once in days or as and when necessary
Harvest	First harvest is at 80 days of planting and subsequent harvests at 45 days interval.
Bio mass yield	The biomass yield 350 tonnes per hectare per year from 6-7 harvests
Intercropping	Intercropped with *Desmanthus* in 3:1 ratio will supply grass and leguminous fodders.

Use in livestock feeding	Hybrid Bajra Napier is the most recommended grass fodder for intensive livestock farming of dairy, sheep and goat farming systems. Chaffed hybrid Napier grass can be fed to dairy animals at the rate of 20-25 kg for dairy cows and buffaloes, 10-15 kg for heifers, 5-10 kg for calves per day per animal. The feeding should be at the rate of 3-5 kg per day per animal for sheep and goats. Chaffing is compulsory in feeding of Hybrid Napier grass as it avoids substantial wastage to the tune of 25 per cent in as such feeding. Routine supplementation of mineral mixture at the rate of 30 grams per day will alleviate ill the effects of oxalates in this grass. The DCP and TDN content of the Hybrid Bajra Napier grass are 7.5 and 70 per cent respectively.

Guinea grass (*Panicum maximum*)	
Synonyms	English: Guinea grass , Hindi: Guinea ghass, Telegu: Guinea gaddi, Tamil: Guinea pul, Kannada: Guinea hallu
Origin	Guinea grass is originated from East Africa, now cultivated widely in tropical and sub tropical regions
Description	It is a perennial crop is erect in growth to a height of 4-6 feet with deep root system. The stem is slender and it develops roots at node when it contact with moist soil. The leaves are long, slender, pale green in colour with hairs. The inflorescence is large, branched and loose panicle
Environment	Guinea grass highly suitable for irrigated farming and desirable temperature range is 25 - 30 degree C. The crop is tolerant to drought, partial shade but it can't withstand water logging. Grows best on deep, fertile, moist soils, but will grow in most soil types provided they are well-drained.
Varieties	Macuenni, Hamil, PGG 1,9,13,14, 19,101, Co 1, 2, Co (GG)3
Field preparation	The land should be prepared to fine tilth by ploughing twice with heavy plough followed by ploughing with cultivator or rotovator and ridges and furrows are prepared for planting
Manures and Fertilizer	Recommended basal application is 25 tonnes of farm yard manure per hectare. Chemical fertilizer is applied at the rate of 60:50:40 kg NPK per ha as basal dose in addition to farm yard manure. Application of 40 kg N per hectare after every cut will sustain the yield on annual basis.
Seed rate and spacing	It can be propagated through seeds and rooted slips. Recommended seed rate is 2.5 kg and root slips is 66,000 Nos. per hectare with the space of 50 x 30 cm.
Irrigation	Irrigation for every 10 days is essential for good yield in irrigated conditions.
Harvest	First harvest at 75 days after planting and subsequent harvest at 45 days interval
Bio mass yield	Bio mass yield is 180 to 200 tonnes per hectare.
Use in livestock feeding	Guinea grass can be fed to all classes of livestock like dairy animals, sheep and goats, horses etc even without chaffing because of its slender and soft stem. The recommended feeding 20 kg for cows, 3-5 kg for sheep and goats and 15-20 kg for horses, 500 gram for rabbits per animal per day. It can also be used for hay or silage with proper preservation methods.

Anjan grass (*Cenchrus ciliaris*)	
Synonyms	English: Cenchrus , Hindi: Anjan or Dhaman, Tamil: Kollukattai pul
Origin	Cenchrus grass is native of Asia, Africa and the Middle East.
Description	Cenchrus grass is an important perennial pasture grass in tropics especially India. The plant grows up to a height of 4-5 feet. The leaves are thick, linear and shiny green or blue in colour and it is a deep rooted grass. It is a crop suitable for erosion control commonly found on the bank of ponds and roadsides. It is not advisable for irrigated farming conditions and cut and carry system of feeding.
Environment	It is pasture grass crop of tropical and sub tropical region. Optimum temperature of 35 degree C for the prosperous growth. It is commonly grown in light, shallow, sandy, rocky and also in calcium rich soil. Its establishment in the heavy clay soil is difficult but when it is established it can withstand all extreme climatic condition. It is a grass of very high drought tolerant and can be grown in areas receiving a very low rainfall of 100 mm per year. It is one of the crop which is tolerant to fire also but cannot withstand water logging
Varieties	Bundel Anjan 1, Bundel Anjan 3, Co-1, Marwar Anjan.
Field preparation	Before the onset of monsoon, proposed pasture land should be prepared to fine tilth.
Manures and Fertilizer	Farm yard manure recommendation for establishment of pasture is 10 tonnes per hectare and NPK fertilizers recommendation is 25: 40: 20 kg per hectare in addition to farm yard manure. In pasture development and maintenance top dressing is not necessary except first year, because grazing animals excretions will act as manure for the same.
Seed rate and spacing	The seed rate is 6 - 8 kg per hectare for pasture establishment. It can also be propagated through root slips at the rate of 40,000 rooted slips with the spacing of 50 x 50 cm. Anjan grass seeds will have seed dormancy and to break dormancy, soak the seeds in 1% potassium nitrate solution for 48 hours and dry the seeds in shades prior to sowing. Direct sowing of old seeds (seeds stored for atlaest one year) will improve the germination, as the storage breaks the dormancy of the seed
Irrigation	In general pasture establishment is aligned with monsoon seasons, there by 5-6 rainy days with the interval of 10 days is essential for growth of grass. However, in short of rainfall, 2-3 irrigations may be offered to complete one cycle of the crop.
Harvest	First cut on 70th or 75th day after sowing and subsequent 4 - 6 cuts depending on growth. However for establishment of pasture, avoiding first cut will cause self seeding, lead good establishment of pasture with density.
Bio mass yield	The bio mass yield is 40 tonnes per hectare per year
Intercropping	Anjan grass can be intercropped with *Stylosanthes spp* at the ratio of 3:1.
Use in livestock feeding	Anjan grass pasture is a potential grazing land for all classes of livestock like dairy animals, sheep and goat. At the same time, it is short height nature and bio mass yield, not recommended for intensive cultivation and cut and carry system of feeding.

Para grass (*Brachiaria mutica*)	
Synonyms	English: Para grass, Hindi : Para Grass, Tamil: Para pul, Kannada: Para hallu
Origin	Para grass is originated from Africa and also called as buffalo grass
Description	It is perennial, semi aquatic and less palatable fodder which grows upright and also it produces runners. It is a vegetatively propagated grass and grows up to a height of 8-10 feet, the leaves are long and narrow.
Environment	It is suitable for cultivation in humid areas. It is grown in seasonally flooded valleys and lowlands as it can withstand water logging and long term flooding.
Varieties	No improved varieties
Field preparation	The field is ploughed accordingly to stagnate the water
Manures and Fertilizer	Farm yard manure is 10 tonnes per hectare before planting and requires about 60:40:40 kg NPK chemical fertilizer per heactare
Seed rate and spacing	Stem cutting of 800-1000 kg is required for one hectare of area and it is planted at the spacing of 60 X 20 cm.
Irrigation	Mostly grown as a rainfed crop, watered every 12-15 days if necessary
Harvest	First cutting after 70-80 days and subsequently after 40-45 days.
Bio mass yield	Biomass yield of Para grass is 80-100 tonnes per hectarea in 4-5 cuttings per year
Use in livestock feeding	Generally, livestock will not relish this grass as it lacks palatability. Adaptation is required for regular feeding of Para grass. Feeding of dairy cows at the rate of 10-15 kg, sheep and goats at the rate of 3-5 kg per animal per day.

Lucerne (*Medicago sativa*)	
Synonyms	English: Lucerne, Hindi: Riska Tamil: Kuthirai masal
Origin	Lucerne otherwise called as Alfalfa is originated from South Central Asia. Because its worldwide distribution and nutritive value it is popularly called as Queen of fodder crop
Description	Lucerne is a leguminous, perennial, semi erect fast growing shrub with trifoliate leaves and spikes of purple with a tap root system. The average height of the plant will be 3 feet with pea type flowers and yellow colour seeds.
Environment	It is the hardy drought tolerant winter season crop and mostly suitable for temperate regions. It can be grown in all types of soil but grown well in drained loamy soil on the other hand Lucerne cannot tolerate water logging
Varieties	LL composite 5, Sirsa 8, Lucerne No 9L, Chetak S 244, Rambler, LL composite 3, IGFRI S 54, IGFRI S 244, Moopa, IGFRI S 112, CO 1 and CO2.

Field preparation	The field is ploughed twice with disc plough followed by ploughing with cultivator until it attains fine tilth. The land is properly levelled and made to beds and channel
Manures and Fertilizer	Farm yard manure can be applied at the rate of 25 tonnes per hectare and chemical fertilizer at the rate of 25:120:40 kg per hectare
Seed rate and spacing	The recommended seed rate is 15 kg per hectare with a solid row spacing of 30 cm at the depth of 2-4 cm. Lucerne seed is very hard in nature and it requires seed treatment like scarification or water soaking over night for proper and uniform germination.
Irrigation	Irrigation is essential for once in 8-10 days or as and when necessary
Harvest	First harvest is at 50-55 days of sowing and the subsequent harvests at 30 days interval
Bio mass yield	Biomass yield of lucerne is 100 tonnes per hectare in a year with 8-10 cuts Since it is perennial crop it can be retained for 3-4 years in the same field.
Intercropping	Not Recommended
Use in livestock feeding	Dairy animals can be fed at the rate of 5-10 kg per animal per day. Small Ruminants can be fed at the rate of 2-3 kg per animal per day. Lucerne hay is desirable fodder for horses at the rate of 4-5 kg per day per animal. Lucerne can also be fed to rabbits at the rate of 500 gram per animal per day. Sudden and excess feeding of Lucerne may cause saponin toxicity symptoms like bloat and nervous signs.

Berseem (*Trifolium alexandrium*)	
Synonyms	English: Berseem , Hindi: Berseem
Origin	Berseem is believed to be native of Mediterranean region and has worldwide distribution as fodder crop
Description	Berseem is one of the important winter crop of Northern India and considering its qualities it is also called as King of fodders. Berseem is a low shrubby annual crop growing 60 – 90 cm high. The main, succulent stem gives off branches terminating in two or three leaves. These stems become fibrous after the flowering stage. Leaves are small, oblong and rounded at the extremities, bright green and slightly hairy.
Environment	Berseem is well adapted to dry and cool climate, preferably cultivated during the winter and spring seasons of north India. It grows very well in the temperature range of 25-30 degree C. On the other hand intensive cold and frost restricting the growth. It grows well in medium to heavy textured soil rich in organic matter, calcium and phosphorous. It remains soft and succulent at all stages of growth.
Varieties	Pusa giant, IGFR-S-99-1, UPB-101,103,104 & 105, Meseavi, BL 11, BL 22, BL 180, BL 42, Hisar Berseem-1, Jawahar Berseem-5, Wardan, JB-1.
Field preparation	The land is prepared to fine tilth by ploughing with heavy plough and it is levelled for proper irrigation. The field may be divided into small beds and channels for better sowing environment

Manures and Fertilizer	Recommended farm yard manure is 15-20 tonnes per hectare. The optimum chemical fertilizer requirement for berseem is 20: 80-90:30 kg NPK per hectare. Top dressing of nitrogen is at the rate of 20 kg per hectare to sustain the yield in subsequent cuttings.
Seed rate and spacing	Desirable seed rate is 25 kg per hectare and with the row spacing of 25 cm.
Irrigation	The crop requires irrigation once in 8-10 days interval and as and when necessary
Harvest	The crop will be ready for first harvest at 55-60 days after sowing and subsequent cuttings at the interval of 30 - 40 days
Biomass yield	Biomass yield is 80 tonnes per hectare per year with 4-5 cuttings
Use in livestock feeding	Berseem is potential leguminous fodder for livestock especially dairy animals in North India and feeding may be at the rate of 10-15 kg per animal per day. Sheep and Goat can be fed at the 2-3 kg per animal per day. The advantage feeding berseem is it will not cause bloat like Lucerne in substantial feed quantity too.

Desmanthus **(*Desmanthus virgatus*)**	
Synonyms	English: Hedge Lucerne , Hindi:Desmanthus Tamil: Velimasal
Origin	Desmanthus is native of North and South America especially Mexico
Description	Desmanthus is prostrate, decumbent perennial shrub of 1 to 1.5 m tall with deep tap root system. The stem is slightly branched, usually glabrous. The leaves are alternate and doubly composite. The flowers are small and grouped into small balls of 5 mm in diameter supported by a long peduncle and the petals are white. The fruit is a linear and flattened pod, where the seeds are more or less diamond-shaped.
Environment	Desmanthus is one of the potential tropical legumes can be effectively grown areas with the average temperature of 30-35 degree C. It can also be called as tropical Lucerne. It can withstand frost and re-growth after getting sufficient moisture. It grows in places where the rainfall ranges from 250 mm to 1600 mm. The crop can withstand moderate drought. Desmanthus can be seen wide range of soil textures from gravel soil to sandy soil and from loam to heavy clay soil.
Varieties	Co 1 and Co 2
Field preparation	The field is prepared to fine tilth by ploughing twice with mould board plough or disc plough twice followed by tilling with cultivator. The field is made into ridges and furrows for good maintenance.
Manures and Fertilizer	The recommended farm yard manure is 25 tonnes per hectare. The chemical fertilizer is 25: 40 : 20 kg NPK per hectare as basal dressing
Seed rate and spacing	Desmanthus seed rate is 20 kg per hectare with solid row spacing of 50 cm. The seeds are very hardy in nature and needs seed treatment before sowing. Seed treatment: Seeds are treated in hot water at 80°C for 5 minutes (boiling water removed from the flame and kept for 4 minutes to attain 80°C). After hot water treatment, seeds should be washed with cold water and soaked in cold water over a night. Seeds should be shade dried before sowing.
Irrigation	Irrigation should be once in a week and as and when necessary in irrigated farming conditions. Intensive cultivation of desmanthus is not recommended for rain fed conditions.

Harvest	First harvest will be at 80 days after sowing and subsequent cuts at the interval of 40 - 45 days
Biomass yield	In intensive cultivation under irrigated conditions, a pure crop yields biomass of about 125 tonnes per hectare
Intercropping	Desmanthus can be effectively intercropped with hybrid Napier bajra grass at 1:3 ratio.
Use in livestock feeding	Desmanthus is a palatable and nutritious legume fodder for all classes of livestock. Feeding shall be 5-10 kg per animal per day for dairy animals, 2-3 kg per animal per day for sheep and goat, 0.5 kg for rabbits. The positive side of Desmanthus feeding is not causing bloat.

Stylo **(*Stylosanthes scabra*)**	
Synonyms	English: Stylo. , Hindi:Stylo, Tamil: Muyalmasal
Origin	Stylosanthes spp. is native of Central and South America
Description	A perennial herb or sub-shrub, semi-erect to erect, with a strong taproot and small round root nodules. Stem much branched, herbaceous or lignified at the base, to 1 m tall. Leaves are trifoliolate, leaflets elliptical Seeds pale brown or purple. Considering it qualities, it is a tropical legume crop suitable for pasture establishment.
Environment	It is a crop of arid and semi arid tropics and it survive well in the temperature range of 25-30 degree C. It is drought resistant hardy species and can be grown in the areas of receiving a minimum rainfall of 450 - 840 mm annually. But it can't tolerate frost and it moderately tolerant to shade and can be grown in silvipasture system.
Field preparation	Plough the field two to three times to obtain good tilth. Land should be prepared as bed and channel for initial establishment of the legume.
Manures and Fertilizer	Recommended farm yard manure is 10 tonnes per hectare at the time of second ploughing. Apply blanket recommendation of 20: 60: 15 kg NPK per hectare in addition to the basal farm yard manure.
Seed rate and spacing	Seed rate of line sowing at the spacing of 30 x 15 cm is 6 kg per hectare and for broadcasting 10 kg per hectare. Seed should be sown at the depth of one cm. Style seeds are hardy in nature and need acid or hot water treatment for good germination. Acid treatment: Dip the seeds in concentrated sulphuric acid for three minutes and wash thoroughly with tap water and presoak the seed in cold water overnight and dry it before sowing. Hot water treatment: Immerse the seeds for 4 minutes in hot water of 80'C and presoak the seeds in cold water overnight before sowing.
Irrigation	Stylo is basically pasture legume and essentially a rainfed crop. But during the period of pasture establishment, care should be taken to provide sufficient irrigation as and when necessary.
Harvest	First cut in taken 70-80 days after sowing and subsequent cuts are taken at an interval of 60-70 days depends on growth.

Bio mass yield	Initial growth and establishment of Stylo will be slow, after establishment through self seeding, it will produce 30 tonnes of biomass yield per hectare.
Intercropping	*Stylosanthes scabra* can be raised as an intercrop with *Cenchrus* in the ratio of 3:1 under rainfed conditions to develop mixed pasture.
Use in livestock feeding	Stylo is a good leguminous fodder suitable for pasture establishment and can be fed to all classes of livestock. Good standing crop can also fed to sheep and goat as cut and carry system of feeding.

Cowpea (*Vigna unguiculata* L. Walp.)	
Synonyms	English: Cow pea, Hindi:Lobia, Tamil: Karamani
Origin	Cowpea is native of southern African regions and is widely grown in Africa, Latin America, and Southeast Asia and in the southern United States. It is chiefly used as a grain crop, fodder and as a vegetable.
Description	Cowpea is an annual, herbaceous legume erect, semi-erect, prostrate, or climbing crop. Growth habit ranges from indeterminate to fairly determinate with the non-vining types tending to be more determinate. The trifoliolate leaves develop alternately. Leaves are smooth, dull to shiny, and rarely pubescent.
Environment	Cowpea is warm season and semi arid crop, where temperature ranging from 20 to 30 degree C. It tolerates heat and dry conditions, but intolerant of frost. Cowpeas are grown under both irrigated and non-irrigated conditions. Cowpea grows on all type of soils and soil conditions, but it grows well on well-drained sandy loams or sandy soils.
Varieties	UPC-618, UPC-625, UPC-622, UPC-628, EC-4216, UPC-287, UPC-5286, GFC-1, GFC-2 and GFC-4, Bundel Lobia - 1,UPC - 287 and UPC - 5286 , Russian Giant, K - 395, IGFRI - 5450 (Kohinoor), C - 88, UPC 5287, UPC – 4200, Co5, Co8
Field preparation	One deep ploughing followed by 2-3 harrowing until attaining fine tilth is essential. In rain fed areas crop can be sown as broadcasting, as irrigated crop the seeds are sown by dibbling method in beds and channel.
Manures and Fertilizer	FYM is required @ 12.5 tonnes per hectare and it is be applied at the time of last ploughing. Chemical fertilizer is applied at the rate of 25:40:20 kg NPK per hectare as basal.
Seed rate and spacing	Seed rate if 40 kg per hectare with the spacing of 30 x 15 cm
Irrigation	This can be grown both as rainfed or irrigated. For irrigated crop, irrigation can be given once in 10-15 days interval.
Harvest	In rainfed conditions, crop is harvested after 50-60 days of sowing or at 50 per cent flowering stage, whereas summer crop should be harvested after 65-70 days of sowing.
Biomass yield	Under irrigated condition, cowpea crop yields 25-30 tonnes per hectare. But under rainfed condition yield level will be 15 to 20 tonnes per hectare.

Use in livestock feeding	Cowpea can be fed all classes of livestock as green and as well dry fodder. However, dry fodder feeding is popular in sheep and goat feeding. It can be fed to the tune of 10 kg per animal per day for large ruminants and 2 per day per animal for small ruminants.

Sesbania (*Sesbania grandiflora*)	
Synonyms	English: Sesbania , Hindi: Sesbania, Tamil: Agathi,
Origin	Sesbania is native of the tropical Asia including, India, Indonesia, Malaysia, Myanmar and Philippines.
Description	It is medium size, fast growing tropical legume tree. The leaves are alternate, pinnate and compound arranged. Flowers may be pink, yellow, light yellow or white in colour. The pods are long, narrow and hanging containing 15-50 red brown kidney shaped seeds.
Environment	It is well adapted to hot and humid environment with temperature of 25-30 degree C with the annual rainfall more than 600 mm. The crop grown in all types of soil but is adopted to grow in saline, alkaline, low fertility and heavy clay soil. It can withstand mild drought too.
Varieties	No improved varieties
Field preparation	Plough two to three times with an iron plough to obtain good tilth. Land can be prepared as ridges and furrows.
Manures and Fertilizer	Single standing of cultivation requires farm yard manure at the rate of 25 tonnes per hectare as basal dressing. Blanket recommendations of 10:25:12.5 kg NPK per hectare chemical fertilizer can be applied in addition to basal dressing of farm yard manure and top dress 12.5 kg Phosphorus once in two years.
Seed rate and spacing	Seed rate is 7.5 kg per hectare and the seeds are sown at a spacing of 100 cm x 100 cm at the side of the ridge at the depth of 5 cm.
Irrigation	The plant is irrigated immediately after sowing and third days after sowing, subsequently once in 15 days interval.
Harvest	The crop will be harvested after eight months after sowing followed by next harvest depends on growth or 60 -80 days once. The tree should not be allowed to flowering and seed setting, as it will reduce the bio mass yield of the crop
Bio mass yield	The biomass yield of about 100 tonnes per can be harvested per year.
Intercropping	It can be effectively intercropped with shade loving crops like guinea grass.
Use in livestock feeding	Sesbania is a nutritious fodder for all classes of livestock especially small ruminants. Dairy animals can be fed at the rate of 10 kg per animal per day and small ruminants at 2-3 kg per animal per day.

Subabul **(*Leucaena leucocephala*)**	
Synonyms	English : Leucaena, Hindi: Subabul, Tamil: Subabul
Origin	Mexico and Central America is the centre of origin of Subabul. The tree-so named for its resemblance to the Babul and tree is quite a common sight in India. This multi-faceted, fast-growing tree was introduced in India from Hawaii, in the early 1980s, for its many benefits. Leucaena provides medium-density wood, high-protein fodder from its leaves and fixes nitrogen in the roots which help the soil.
Common name	Wild tamarind, White babool, Lead tree, Ipil-Ipil
Description	It is evergreen tree and it can withstand prolonged drought or frost by defoliation and recover to normal growth under favourable conditions. The flowers are small, white globular and are self–pollinated, pods are cluster, thin, flat and straight. Each pod contain 15-30 seeds, mature seeds are flat, shiny brown and have waxy seed coat.
Environment	Subabul is cultivated widely in the tropics as a fodder plant, especially on dry waste lands. Subabul is well grown in area where the temperature range of 22-45^{0}C with a rainfall of 600-1700 mm in an altitude upto 1000m. It is found to grow on diverse soil types. It can be grown in neutral to alkaline soil and it can't withstand acidic soil. Soil with high Ca and P is preferred. Subabul (kubabul) trees are grown all over India.
Varieties	Cunningham, K8, K28, K67, K636, Co1, Hawaiian giant, Giant Ipil-Ipil, Pudhiya soundal and hybrids 'KX2' and 'KX3'
Field preparation	The field is prepared to fine tilth and it can be made into bed and channels or ridges and furrows.
Manures and Fertilizer	About 25 tonnes of FYM is applied and mixed to the soil at the time of last ploughing. Chemical fertilizers are given at the rate of 10:60:30 kg NPK /ha.
Seed rate and spacing	Pre-sowing treatment: Seeds have hard waxy seed coat which is impervious to water hence need pre-sowing treatment to ensure uniform germination Mechanical scarification: It is done by putting seed in a rotating drum lined with sand paper or knicked mechanically by knife or scissors Acid treatment: Immerse seeds in concentrated H2SO4 or HCl for 15 minutes, washing and drying seeds before used for sowing Hot water treatment: Seeds treated with hot water (80%) for 3-4 minutes gives about 80% germination. A seed rate of 3-4 kg is recommended for nursery planting in polythene bags. The seedlings are transplanted to main field during the onset of monsoon when it is 1.5 to 3 months old or with 6-8 leaves. For direct sowing a seed rate of 10kg/ha is required and it is sown in thes spacing of 100X 30cm for fodder crop.
Irrigation	Generally irrigation is not required since it is planted in rainfed condition, but can be irrigated during severe dry period. For irrigated crop the field has to be irrigated once in 10-15 days.

Harvest	The crop will be ready for first cutting as early as 6 months after planting the seeds. The initial cutting should not be done until the trunk has attained atleast 3 cm diameter thickness and the subsequent cutting on 60 – 80 days interval depends on the growth
Bio mass yield	Under irrigated condition tree yields about 90-100t/ha and in rainfed crop tree yields about 40 t/ha. Subabul contains 26% CP. Thus it is a good source of energy and protein. Subabul contain toxic principle Mimosine which has adverse effect on growth, reproduction and health of animals. Mimosine may cause loss of hairs in young cattle. So it should be used as per recommended levels. The addition of iron salts decreases mimosin toxicity.
Intercropping	It can be intercropped with an cereal or grass fodder only for first year after the shade loving crops like guinea grass can be grown.
Use in livestock feeding	It is good leguminous fodder tree and leaves are good source of protein for all classes of ruminants. Periodical lopping of branches of trees will offer reasonable biomass of tree fodder. Palatability of the tree leaves is also good.
Feeding of livestock	Cattle can be 5 kg of tree leaves per animal per day. Sheep and Goat can be fed 2 kg tree leaves per animal per day.

Glyricidia (***Glyricidia sepium***)	
Synonyms	English: Glyricidia , Hindi: Glyricidia , Tamil : Glyricidia
Origin	Glyricidia is a small size tropical tree and native of Mexico.
Description	It is a fast growing leguminuous tree to a height up to 7-10 m, has a medium crown. The tree has deep roots and the leaves are alternate and pinnate with papery, oblong leaflet. Flowers are short usually pink, to whitish-brown and it is hermaphrodite in nature and is strongly out crossing with a robust self-incompatibility mechanism. It is insect pollinated and mostly by black bee. Pods are dehiscent, pale green or reddish-pink when unripe, turning pale yellow-brown when fully ripe.
Environment	It grows well in warm seasonally dry climate with moderate annual rainfall. It grows in temperature of 27-35 degree C. It can be effectively grown in deep, well drained, medium textured fertile soil. It can tolerate fire and the tree sprout when the rainfall arrives
Varieties	There are no formally recognized varieties
Field preparation	Field is generally prepared to deep fine tilth.
Manures and Fertilizer	Generally not recommended
Seed rate and spacing	The tree can be propagated both vegetative and sexual method through stem cutting and seeds and growth in stem cuttings will be faster than seed. It is planted at a spacing of 3-5 feet distance and it can be grown in the boundaries of the field. Gliricidia stem cutting or 3-4 month old seedlings can be planted on buds at 50 cm spacing during the rainy season. For steep slopes, closer plant spacing of is recommended for better soil erosion control.

Irrigation	The tree are planted during rainy season and the irrigation is not required
Harvest	The crop can be harvested once in year for the first two years and after that once in three months interval based on the bio mass yield
Bio mass yield	Crop yields about 9 tonnes per hectare fodder.
Intercropping	In widely spaced tree crops guinea grass can be successfully intercropped. It is also highly useful as fence crops in agricultural fields.
Use in livestock feeding	G. sepium being a leguminous fodder rich in protein and can be offered ruminants especially small ruminants. However, it will not be readily relished by the animals and needs some adaptation period for feeding the same. Wilting the fodder will improve the intake of the animals.

Mulberry (*Morus alba*)	
Origin	Mulberry is native of China. Mulberry is a good fodder for silkworm rearing and traditionally being cultivated for that purpose
Description	Mulberry is a multipurpose perennial small size tree grows up to 15 feet height with tan gray ridged trunk and light green leaves, which are arranged alternatively and are lobed or unlobed, cordate, dentate or tapering. The trees produce small green-yellow flowers in dense spikes and an oval aggregate fruit.
Environment	Mulberry can be grown in tropical and sub tropical regions. It is moderately tolerant to drought and hardy to cold. It can be grown in deep loam soil with good drainage and it requires supplemental irrigation at the times of short of rainfall.
Varieties	Kanva 2, MR 2, S 30, S 36, S 54, DD (Viswa), V1, S 13, S 34, RFS 135, RFS 175, S 1635
Field preparation	The field should be prepared with heavy implements for two times followed by cultivator ploughing for two times to fine tilth. Ridges and furrows are formed for planting mulberry saplings
Manures and Fertilizer	Farm yard manure is applied at the rate of 25 tonnes per hectare and should be incorporated with soil at the last ploughing. Chemical fertilizer is applied at the rate of 300:120:120 kg NPK per hectare in split doses. Apply the first dose of fertilizers three months after planting. Follow subsequent fertilizer application after each leaf harvest and pruning. .
Seed rate and spacing	Mulberry tree can be propagated through seeds, cuttings and by grafting. The plants are grown in nursery up to 90 days and the transplanted to the main field with the spacing of 60 X 60 or 90 X 90 cm in ridges and furrows.
Irrigation	The crop has to be irrigated depends on the crop need, may be once in 10-15 days.
Harvest	The crop can be harvested once in three months at 5 feet above the ground level.
Bio mass yield	The average yield of mulberry leaves is 35-40 tonnes per hectare.
Intercropping	It can be intercropped with small duration crop like cowpea
Use in livestock feeding	Leaves of mulberry is a palatable and nutritious tree fodder for all classes of livestock especially small ruminants. Sheep and Goat can be fed 2-5 per day per animal for good growth.

Fodders Gallery

Fodder Maize

Fodder Sorghum

Fodder Bajra

Fodder Sorghum (Multi cut)

Bajra Napier cross

***Cenchrus* Grass**

Guinea Grass

Para Grass

Lucerne

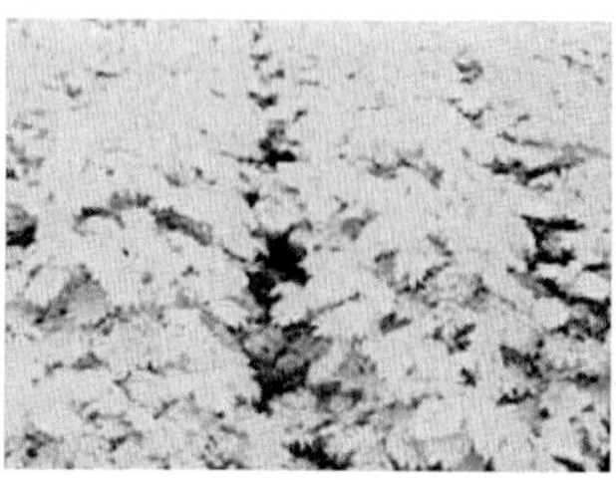

Hedge Lucerne

Berseem

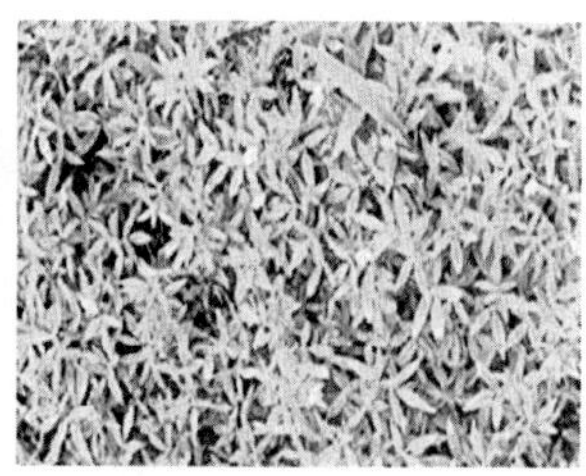

Stylosanthes

Sesbania

Leucaena

Glyricidia

Clitoria Ternatea

Clitoria is native to tropical Asia. It is also called as Butterfly pea, Aparjita. The butterfly pea *(C. ternatea)* is a deep-rooted, tall slender, climbing legume with five leaflets and have different colours of flowers. It grows in tropical climate with prolonged drought. The crop can be grown well in the annual rainfall of 700 to 1500 mm and from sea level up to an altitude of 1600-1800 m. It is well adapted to a variety of soil types but is particularly adapted to shallow, heavy clay and sodic soils (pH 5.5-8.9) including calcareous soils. Propagation is through seed, also produces seed continuously. Butterfly pea is productive type of fodder and may be grown with other grasses in the pasture. The production of forage was 25-29 ton DM/ha and dry matter digestibility levels vary between 60-75%. Improved varieties are IGFRI-S-23-1 and IGFRI-S-12 available for forage cultivation in India.

Siratro *(Macroptelium atropurpureum)*

Sirarto is originated from Central America. It is hardy drought tolerant deep rooted perennial legume suited to a wide range of well drained soils. Non-bloating highly palatable, productive and persistant ideal for grazing. It is widely adopted to soils of different textures and pH levels including saline soils. It can be grown in area receiving rainfall of 700 mm to 1500 mm but cannot withstand flooding and waterlogging. It prefers warm areas with mean annual temperatures ranging from 22°C to 30°C. Siratro is a creeping or climbing legume, with bright green leaves between 2–7 cm long, with each leaf having three broad leaflets. The two lower leaflets will often have an extra rounded lobe, and the leaves have silky hairs on their underside. 'Sweet pea-like' dark red-purple flowers are borne on long spikes most of the year. After flowering, narrow pods 5–10 cm long. Dry matter yields are mostly in the range of 5–10 tonnes per hectare per year.

Scarcity Fodders

The unique feature of Indian livestock farming system is its wide feed resource base consists of compounded feed, irrigated and rain fed fodder, pasture and grazing lands grasses and legumes, tree leaves and residues of various crops. Considering the livestock population size of India, feed resources are always on scarce side especially during lean seasons. During scarce seasons like non agri seasons, floods, drought etc., the feed resources of low nutritive and economic value can be used to sustain the farming systems and those feed resources are called scarcity fodder or unconventional feed resources. The characteristics of scarcity fodders are that they are generally end products of agriculture and agri food processing and not fit for human consumption. They are also generally high fibre feed resources which will try to fill the stomach of animals with least cost input. In scarcity fodder, sugarcane tops, banana stems and leaves, papaya leaves, Casava leaves, vegetable crop residues (Cabbage, Cauliflower, Carrot, Potato etc) are promising feed resources as green roughages. Sugarcane bagasse, soybean hulls, paper waste, fallen tree leaves and saw dust are promising dry roughages of scarcity fodder. Though scarcity fodders can be used effectively for animal feeding care should be taken considering its daily intake quantity, because of the reason that, most of the scarcity fodders has some form of ant nutritional factors causing adverse effects in high intake. Considering the same, adaptation time is required with incremental increase in feeding with a maximum threshold.

Grassland and Pasture Management

Grasslands, rangelands, grazing lands and pasture constitute a vast cover of the earth's surface as natural or artificial vegetation and supporting livestock grazing. All through the world, in extensive livestock farming system, allowing the animal for grazing is a way feeding the same cost effectively. The major species depends on grazing for feeding are *cattle*, buffalo, sheep and goat. In addition to that grasslands are important part in eco systems, which support the diversity of plants and animals in earth. Though we are commonly using the worlds like grassland, range lands, pasture etc, it is have clear differences among them.

Grassland is a land with more than 75 per cent cover by grasses. The examples of Grasslands are Western Hirnalayan pastures, semiarid grasslands of Western and Central India, in shrub lands of fthe Deccan Plateau and the grass lands of Shola forests of the Western Ghats, Nilgiri forest ranges.

Rangeland is a piece of vegetation which may be of grasses, legumes, shrubs and fodder or multipurpose trees, wherein grazing can occur. Pasture is a piece of land in which grasses are grown or cultivated and managed for feeding livestock. It is mostly artificial in nature through proper management of vegetation and grazing. Sometimes the properly managed grasslands with high yielding species of grass, legumes and good soil fertility are also known as pasture. The composition and the quality of grasslands vary with different soil and climatic variables of the grassland.

Pastures are generally established and managed by human intervention for optimum production. Though like western countries, pastures are not available in India in large scale for livestock grazing, grazing lands are available in different type of lands.

1) Village grazing lands - The common property village lands, now owned by private are used animal grazing called village grazing lands.
2) Grazing lands at embankments – Sides of river, lakes, ponds, water bodies will have vegetation for grazing due to sufficient sub soil moisture
3) Grazing lands at bunds of crop fields – Bunds of various crop fields will have vegetation for grazing
4) Hill slope and Fallow grazing lands – They are the grazing lands available in the various hill slopes and permanent or current fallow lands

In Indian livestock farming scenario, natural grasslands and pastures are playing a critical role because they are forming the cheapest feed resources for grazing livestock. Yet, the quality of grasslands and pastures is not good always because of two main reasons namely over grazing and poor management. Conservation of grasslands is becoming order of the day, because of its role in nomadic and extensive livestock farming systems. The basic approaches in grassland and pasture management are ecological succession, assisted ecological and intensive management. Ecological succession is a natural process of vegetation development and maintenance and it is time consuming process. In assisted ecological, improving the fertility of soil, water conservation and seeding are the techniques. In Intensive management, standard practices are followed for proper growth of local specific and selected plant species in the grassland cum pasture, controlled grazing methods are also employed in this approach. The strategy for good grassland and pasture management consists of following series of activities.

- Protection from grazing – Fencing with cost effective materials plays a major role in protection from grazing and it will prevents the access for livestock for grazing
- Soil and water conservation – It includes all the soil and water conservation technologies like provision of bunds, contour bunds, trenches etc to prevent the runoff especially in slope grasslands and pastures
- Bush cleaning- Clearing of unwanted plant species from the grasslands on continuous basis. Lopping of over grown trees to avoid shading for grass growth.
- Re-seeding – Seeding of selected grass and legumes suitable for pasture will improve the quality of pasture. Cenchrus , Guinea, Stylo, Siratro spp may be selected based on the climate of the region

- Fertilizer application- Application blanket recommendation of farm yard manure, or nitrogen etc will improve the growth of plant species
- Mixed Stands – Mixed seeding of grass and legumes will improver the soil fertility and bio mass yield in terms of protein per unit land.

Grazing Management

The single most dominant for deterioration of grassland and pasture is over grazing. Sometimes overgrazing will offer the time for the plants to rejuvenate itself for next season growth and soil become infertile. Considering that a number of grazing methods are being employed in pasture management.

Continuous controlled grazing - In this method, continuous grazing is allowed but at the same time, number of animals or duration of grazing is controlled to avoid over grazing. Sometimes grassland and pastures are divided in to paddocks and controlled grazing is allowed based on the growth of vegetation.

Deferred grazing - In these methods, pastures are divided in to paddocks, in selected paddocks animals will be allowed for grazing and others will put on rest based on the growth especially during lean seasons like summer. The resting time will allow the plants to rejuvenate themselves for next season growth.

Rotational grazing - In this method, pastures are divided in to paddocks and animals will be allowed to graze in one paddock at a time for a short period. Then it will be moved to second and third paddocks. After a cycle is over, process will be repeated.

Deferred rotational grazing - It is combination of rotational grazing and deferred grazing in which rotational grazing is practiced at deferred periods. It is the most effective methods which will avoid over grazing, water runoff and will improve the soil structure, fertility and growth of vegetation.

Hohenheim system - It is a grazing system followed in Germany during emergency times. In this systems, pasture is divided in to paddocks and animals divided in to lot based on its production stage like for cows, early, mid, late lactation, dry cows, growing animals etc. Based on the priority, a particular lot will allowed to graze in one paddock for some time followed by next priority lot animals. Generally, early lactating and mid lactating and growing animals will be getting first preference for grazing followed by other of animals in the same paddock.

Cut and Carry or Zero grazing - . In this method, animals will not be allowed for grazing, but grass, legumes and other fodders will be cut by the farmers especially by women fold, carry them to the stalls of the animals for feeding. It is also called Cut and Carry system of feeding and popular in India. Rigorous cutting even during lean seasons like summner as well winter in high altitude regions will affect the vegetation and will adversely affect the quality of pasture or grazing lands. Application of manure will be additional process, because this system prevents the dropping animal manure in the field. In cut and carry system pasture, mostly intensive pasture crop production is carried out for efficiency of production.

Carrying Capacity

Carrying capacity of the pasture or grasslands is a function of mainly two variable namely, bio mass yield of pasture and quantity of dry matter intake by the animals. Bio mass yield of pasture will depend on type of vegetation, species vegetation, its growth potential, soil fertility, water conservation etc. Quantity of dry matter intake will depend on type of animal, production function like growth, lactation, pregnancy etc. Here, number of animal allotments per unit of land is called stocking rate. Stocking rate is number of animals allotted for grazing per hectare of grassland or pasture. Both biomass yield and stocking rate are dynamic in nature depending on the season and stage of production function of animals. Naturally carrying capacity will also be dynamic depending on the season and type of livestock allowed for grazing. Based on that, carrying capacity needs to be properly optimized for effective grazing management to maintain a sustainable pasture production and livestock growth. If several species of livestock are allowed for grazing to make common indicator, all the livestock can be converted in to Animal Unit or Adult Cow Unit for expressing the carrying capacity.

Grasslands and pastures are integral part of Indian livestock farming system, proper preservation of natural grasslands and pasture are essential for cost effective livestock production especially for small and marginal famers. For effective conservation of the same, community participation is mandatory. Keeping that in mind, all the grassland and pasture management strategies should be inclusive of all the stakeholders like government, community, livestock farmers for effective implementation.

Activity

1) Test harvest the fodders of your farm and offer your comments
2) Feed the various fodders of your farm to the livestock and offer your comments
3) Design model fodder plot for your farm
4) List the scarcity fodders available in your farm
5) Make a visit to the grazing land of your farm and prepare a forage inventory

Exam Corner

1. What is forage?
2. What is fodder?
3. List some cereal fodders
4. List some leguminous fodders
5. List some grass fodders
6. What is annual fodder?
7. What is perennial fodder?
8. List some grass and legumes suitable for pasture
9. Difference between grassland and pasture
10. What is deferred grazing?
11. What is rotational grazing?
12. What is cut and carry system of feeding

8

Fodder Preservation

Learning Objectives

- Explain the concept of fodder preservation and its need
- Discuss the purpose of hay making and its benefits
- Details silage making process and its advantages

The key characteristic of monsoon based agriculture of India is variability of availability of forage and fodder resources for livestock. In monsoon seasons, fodder availability will be at its peak, and the same will be scarce in dry months. Considering that, preservation of fodder during monsoon months especially through rainfed farming is essential to ensure a fodder supply throughout the year. Preservation of fodder is process of preserving the excess available fodder in a proper form without the loss of nutrients and its palatability. Based on the methods, preservation can be classified in to two namely dry and green preservation, in former, controlled loss of moisture is essential to minimize the nutrient loss and in later, preserving the moisture and nutrients to a desirable extent is the challenge. The two promising methods of fodder preservation are hay making for dry preservation and silage making for green preservation.

Hay Making

Hay making is a process of preservation of green fodder by drying process. The term hay denotes the immature dried green fodders like grass, legumes and cereal fodders at the dry matter content of 85-90 per cent. The most suitable fodders are various grasses, cereal and leguminous fodders like Lucerne, Sorghum and Berseem. The fodder should be cut before maturity spread over a place in rows and put on hay racks for sun shine drying. Flowering or fifty per cent flowering is suitable for quality hay making. The characteristics of quality hay are soft, pliable, free from any off odours, retention of green colour of the crop and minimum loss of leaves due to shattering and it should not have more than 15 per cent moisture.

The cultivated fodder crops which are having soft stems are more suitable for hay making, oats, sorghum varieties with soft stems, berseem, lucerne, cenchrus grass, guinea grass and other natural grasses for highly preferred for hay making. Chopping is recommended for hard stem fodders. The purpose of hay making is to preserve the green fodder by keeping is moisture content below 20 per cent through sunshine drying there by preventing the action of plant and bacterial enzymes on the plant nutrients. Moreover, drying to the tune of 80-85 per cent dry matter will avoid the fermentation process, will normally happen in the storage of green fodder. Twisting the stems of green fodder will indicate the moisture content of the fodder. Six hours of drying for two days with a total of 12 hours is sufficient for good hay making. In Indian farming conditions, hay racks, shattering floors, hay sheds are also preferable for hay making process. Controlled sun shine drying will prevent the loss of nutrients from hay and proper handling of cut fodder will avoid the shattering of leaves. Avoiding rain exposure of hay in the making process will prevent the leeching loss of nutrients. The hay can be stored in hay racks.

Silage Making

Feed is the major cost in any livestock feeding. In dairy cattle, buffalo and small ruminants feeding, feeding of good quality green roughages in the form of green grass, cereals and leguminous fodders will substantially reduce the use of concentrates or compounded feeds, thereby reduce the cost of production of milk or meat. Cost of grains and oil cakes are also in the in the escalating trend from time to time, which necessitates not only effective production of green fodders, and also efficient use of the same for economy of production. Moreover, availability of green fodder in the lean seasons is a critical issue in India, where agriculture heavily depends on monsoon rain. Considering that, silage making is a promising green fodder preservation process to be recommended for practice in every livestock farm.

Silage

Silage is a preserved green fodder through anaerobic fermentation having the moisture content of 60-70 per cent. The green fodders rich in readily available sugars especially cereal fodders like maize or sorghum are highly suitable for silage making. In this anaerobic process, sugars of the fodders are converted in to lactic acid, that itself will act as a preservative for the green fodder and food material for rumen microbes.

Silo

The structure in which green fodder is preserved is called Silo. Silos may be of Trench or Pit type or Surface silo. Surface silo is cost friendly than pit silo and ease for management. Pit silo or trench silo should be constructed in an elevated place of the farm and it should be free from water logging in rainy seasons. Construction of silo is the first step in silage making and one cubic meter of silo space can store around 500 kg of chaffed green fodder. In a pit silo, steps should be provided to get in to the bottom with ease by the workforce and bottom made of concrete floor is highly preferable.

Preparation of Silage

1. Cereal fodders at the flowering stage or milk stage is ideal for silage making
2. Harvest the fodder at 30-35 per cent dry matter
3. Wilt the cut fodder for half a day in sun shine to minimize the moisture
4. Chaff the fodder in to 2-3 cm size material
5. Fill the chaffed fodder in to the silo tightly
6. Press and fill the fodder layer by layer of 20-25 cms thickness
7. Use preservatives and additives in layer by layer filling up
8. Salt at the rate of 8 kg per ton of fodder can be added as preservative
9. Molasses or Jaggery water can be added at the rate of 20 kg per ton for readily available sugars in case grass fodder silage
10. Molasses is not essential for cereal fodders in silage making
11. Filling and pressing should be in one go quick process
12. After filling, cover the top layer with non specific dried grass
13. Seal the silo with polythene sheet and put weight or sand
14. Make a slope in the top of the silo for rain water drain
15. Maintain the silo as such for period of minimum 45 days
16. Open the silo, check for any fungus growth and feed the quality silage to animals

Characteristics of Good Silage

Quality silage should be firm textured soft material, bright yellow or greenish brown in colour with strong lactic acid odour and it should free from ammonia or butyric acid odour. Quality silage will have moisture of 60-70 per cent, pH of 4-4.5 and a mean lactic acid of 8-10 per cent.

Constraints in Silage Making

Availability of fodder for silage making will be in the South west or North east monsoon months. The incessant rainfall in monsoon months will interrupt the process of silage making. Moreover, silage making in a silo is a one go process, it cannot be intermittent. The critical steps in silage making are wilting, pressing, packing and covering the fodder without any external moisture from rain. Considering that utmost care should be taken in silage process with sufficient labour and inputs for harvesting, filling, packing and covering the same.

Feeding of Silage

Feeding of silage is similar to green fodder. Dairy cattle, buffalo may be fed at the rate of 15 to 20 kg per animal per day. Sheep and goats may be fed at the rate of 3-5 kg kg per animal per day. However, feeding of silage should be smooth, initial adaption period of one week should be given at the rate of 5 kg and 1 kg per animal per day for large and small ruminants. Increase in quantity in silage feeding should be incremental and smooth to avoid any digestive problems. Considering the cost economics of silage preparation, silage feeding is one of the promising preservation strategies not only to handle the lean season shortages but also to preserve excess available green fodder at the end of monsoon seasons.

Activity

1. Calculate the cost of production of one tone of hay and silage making
2. Prepare five kg of silage with polythene bag method and test the quality of the same after 45 days of storage

Exam Corner

1. What is fodder preservation?
2. What is hay?
3. What is silage?
4. Difference between hay and silage
5. Difference between hay and straw
6. What is silo?
7. What is ideal stage of harvest for silage making?
8. What is wilting in silage making?

9. List the constraints in silage making
10. What is the function of molasses in silage making?
11. List the fodder crops suitable for silage making
12. Characteristics of good silage

9

Agro Forestry

Learning Objectives

- Explain the concept of agro forestry and its uses
- Discuss the classification of various agro forestry models
- Details the concept of animal agro forestry and its advantages

As per Food and Agriculture Organization (FAO), agro forestry represents land-use systems and technologies where trees, shrubs, palms, bamboos, etc. are deliberately used on the same land-management units as agricultural crops and or animals, in some form effective utilization of land and to increase the returns per unit of land. The three main components of agro forestry are land, crops & trees and animals and that can be combined in numerous spatial and temporal function thus creating different kinds of production function.

Land is the basic component in any agro forestry model, though agro forestry is suitable any land holdings, small and marginal land holdings are highly appropriate, considering the objective of improved productivity per unit of land. It is also suitable for problematic soils and soils which are susceptible to soil erosion. Considering the objective of agro forestry the main components are land, crops and livestock of which crops may be agricultural or horticultural or forestry crops or grazing land management in the name of pasture for animal feeding or combination of above in various patterns.

Selection of crops requires a careful application of mind based on knowledge of the various crops, adaptations, production uses, as well as family needs, opportunities for trade and markets. Any farm animal can be used in agro forestry systems. The choice of animal will be based on the value the farmer places on animal-derived benefits including income, food, labour, non-food products, use of crop residues and manure. Classification of agro forestry is as follows,

Structural Classification

Structural composition indicates the nature of components like agricrops, horticrops, forestry crops, pasture, grass land etc with or without animal component.

1. Agrosilvicultural system: It is the combination of agriculture and silvicultural crops. One of the sub classifications of this agro forestry model is horti pastural in which horticultural crops integrated with pasture component with livestock.
2. Silvipastural system: It is a combination of forestry crops with pasture or grazing land for integrating livestock as component.
3. Agrosilvopastural system:- Combination of Agri, Silvi, and Pasture component with livestock integration.
4. Silviculture: It is the management of forest trees to yield timber, industrial woods, fire wood, fuel wood, and medicine etc.

Functional Classification

It is based on the function of the agro forestry model like food, fodders, timber, fuel wood and other functions.

1. Productive agroforestry:- It indicates the production of essential commodities required to meet the basic needs of the society. The productive functions are supply of food, fodder, timber and fuel wood and other products
   a. Protective Agro forestry: - This system refers to protect the land, to improve climate, reduce wind and water erosion, improve soil fertility, provide shelter etc. The protective functions are Windbreak, Shelterbelts, Soil and moisture Conservation, Soil improvement and Shade (for crop, animals and man)
   b. Multipurpose agro forestry system: it ensures multipurpose production through optimizing both productive and protective function eg. hedge row intercropping, home garden.

Ecological Classification

In ecological classification, agro forestry can be classified as tropical, sub tropical, temperate based on their climate of the area in which agro forestry models being developed.

Socio-economic Classification

In social economic classification, agro forestry models are classified based on the farming class of individual and the objective of the same. Three major socio economic classifications are Subsistence agro forestry (mostly for livelihoods of marginal and small farming systems), Commercial agro forestry (large commercial plantation of forest tree with high timber value, economic value etc), and Intermediate agro forestry which serves in intermediate way of above systems.

Animal Agroforestry

Animal agroforestry refers to the system of land use which cultivation of various crops (agri, horti, forestry crops) and integrating livestock with them and offers various advantages. It not provides food for people and but also offers fodders for livestock rearing. Integrating livestock provides additional income opportunities for the farmers and increase the income per unit area of land. Integration of livestock will also offers organic manure for crops and improve the soil fertility in long run. This model highly suitable for the social life of rural farmers and mitigate the risk in dry land agriculture due to unpredicted climatic conditions. Further, animal agro forestry system being economical, environmentally friendly and helps in enhancing both food and forage production simultaneously from the same unit of land and sparing of land for exclusive forage and fodder production is not necessary which alleviates the pressure on sole livestock farming systems. Various models of livestock integrated agro forestry are as follows,

1. Silvipastoral system (forestry + pasture + livestock).
2. Agrisilvipastoral system (agriculture + forestry + pasture + livestock).
3. Horti-pastoral system (orchards + pasture+ livestock).

Advantages of Agroforestry

- Production of diverse products
- Improve the efficiency of utilization of land
- Improves soil nutrient and fertility
- Prevents water erosion and improves water table
- Lower the use of agrochemicals
- Improves microclimatic condition
- Improve the income per unit of land
- Improvement in wildlife and pollinator habitat
- Increase carbon sequestration

Disadvantage of Agroforestry

- Labour intensive system
- Takes long time for pay back
- Limited possibilities for sell all the product
- Lack of legal support for agro forestry farmers
- Competition of resources
- Allelopathy effects

Activity

1. Design a silvi-horti- pasture agro forestry model for two acres for your farm and workout the inputs and budget for the same
2. Design a silvi pasture agro forestry model of one acre for rural small ruminant production system and workout the inputs and budget for the same

Exam Corner

1. What is agro forestry?
2. What are the components of agro forestry?
3. What is structural classification in agro forestry?
4. What is silviculture in agro forestry?
5. What is silvipasture in agro forestry?
6. What is hortipasture in agro forestry?
7. What is hortisilvipasture in agro forestry
8. What is ecological classification in agro forestry?
9. What is animal agro forestry?
10. List the advantages of agro forestry
11. Socio economic classification in agro forestry
12. What is multipurpose agro forestry?

10

Labour Management in Livestock Farms

Learning Objectives

- Explain the role of labour management in livestock farms
- Discuss the labour forecasting for livestock farms
- Discuss the labour input for various activities of livestock farms

In economics, labour is defined as manual or mental work for acquiring income for their livelihoods. In farming domain, the agriculture labor is defined as labourers who earn their main source of income by working in farms of others for a wage. In this type, labours may classified in three namely skilled, semi skilled and unskilled labours based on their skill sets.

Skilled labour is a type of labour, who is having specific skills like carpentry, black smiths, drivers, masonry etc will be utilized to perform a specific function, and correspondingly their wages will be on the higher side than other two types. Semi skilled labours are those having some period of experience in carrying out agriculture field works; however it may not require specific skill set to perform that function, except of period of experience. Unskilled labour constitutes the remaining labour force, who is involved in various agriculture day to day agriculture farming activities.

In general, the livestock farm will have all these three labour categories for the routine function of the farm. Here, farm managers should keep in mind that, in any livestock farm, labour cost is the second largest cost item after feeding cost of livestock. Labour forecasting for routine and special functions, allotment, getting the work done by the labour, fixing and time to time revision of wages for various types of labour, budgeting for the labour are the duties of the farm manager.

In a multi species livestock farm, the farm manager will be assigned the job of labour allotment and management for various sections of the farms including the fodder production. Considering that, a farm manager may be an agriculture science graduate or animal science graduate should aware of the positive labour management strategies to manage the labour efficiently to optimize the production efficiency.

Labour Forecasting

Labour forecasting is the process of calculating the labour requirements for the various functions like fodder cultivation, irrigation, harvest, chaffing the fodder and other functions of various livestock units of the farms like dairy, sheep and goat, piggery, poultry and rabbitery etc. The forecast of the labour may be for a month or for a whole year to calculate the budget requirements of the farm. Calculation of labour requirements will also be helpful in establishment of new farms and getting sanction for labour allotment. At times, farm manager will also be required to forecast the labour requirement for special operations like sowing, silage and hay making, summer ploughing, new field establishments etc. The simple method of forecasting labour requirements is expressing the number of labour requirements in "man days" for a activity on prescribed unit basis, which is applicable to both gender.

Labour Requirements

Labour requirements for various activates of the farm in terms of man days per unit activity are summarized below for use. Here, unit activity will vary with type of farm operations. For an example, number of man days requirement for establishing a field will be for a hectare or acre, for harvest of fodder will be for a ton of fodder, for milking the cows will be for litre of milk etc.

Sl.No.	Activity	Labour requirements (Man days)
	Fodder Production	
1.	Preparation of new agriculture fields	20 per hectare
2.	Ploughing of agricultural fields (Tractor)	
3.	Planting of hybrid Napier stems	20 per hectare
4.	Broadcasting of cereal fodders	05 per hectare
5.	Sowing of leguminous fodders	20 per hectare
6.	Irrigation of fodder fields	02 per hectare
7.	Manuring of fodder fields	08 per hectare
8.	Harvesting of hybrid Napier fodder	30 per hectare
9.	Harvesting of leguminous fodder	30 per hectare
10.	Harvesting of cereal fodders	30 per hectare
11.	Silage making (excluding the harvest)	06 per 10 tonnes
12.	Hay making (excluding the harvest)	06 per 10 tonnes
13.	Weeding in fodder plots	30 per hectare
14.	Cleaning of fodder fields	20 per hectare
15.	Seed collection of leguminous fodders	40 per hectare

16.	Seed collection of cereal fodders	24 per hectare
17.	Stem cuttings in hybrid Napier grass	01 per 1500 slips
18.	Establishment of pasture	05 per hectare
19.	Nursery raising of fodder trees	100 bags per day per person
20.	Seed cleaning	12 per hectare
21.	Chaffing of fodder	01 per tonne

Dairy Section		**Labour Requirement (Man days)**
	Dairy animal shed cleaning and maintenance	01 per 10 adult animals
	Milking (Manual)	01 per 50 litres milk
	Milking (Machine)	01 per 100 litres milk
	Grazing of cattle or buffalo	01 per 40 adult animals

Sheep and goat section		**Labour Requirement (Man days)**
	Grazing of animals	01 per 50 adult animals
	Sheep shed management	01 per 100 adult animals
	Weighment of animals	03 per 150 adult animals
	Deworming and vaccination	02 per 200 adult animals
	De ticking	04 per 200 adult animals

Piggery section		**Labour Requirement (Man days)**
1	Pig shed management – for a unit size 1+10 and its off springs with concentrate feeding, power sprayer for cleaning	01
2	Pig shed management – for a unit size 1+10 and its off springs with swill feeding and manual cleaning	02

Poultry section		**Labour Requirement (Man days)**
1	Broiler farm (Deep litter house with automation in watering)	01 per 3000 birds
2	Country chicken farm (Deep litter house with automation in watering)	01 per 2000 birds
3	Commercial layer farm (Cage housing, automation in feeding and watering)	01 per 10,000 birds
4	Egg collection on commercial layer farm	02 per 10000 eggs
5	Broiler breeder farm (Cage housing-excluding Artificial Insemination)	02 per 2000 birds
6	Layer breeder farm (Cage housing – Excluding Artificial Insemination)	02 per 2000 birds
7	Japanese quail breeder or layer farm (Cage housing)	01 per 5000 birds

	Poultry section	Labour Requirement (Man days)
8	Japanese quail farm for meat – (Deep litter house with automation in watering)	01 per 5000 birds
	Feed Mills	
1	Preparation of compounded feed (Batch weighing to packing of feed)	02 per ton of feed

Based on the above table, farm manager can forecast the requirement of labour for a short period daily or week basis or for longer period like monthly and yearly basis and it will also help in forecasting the budget requirement for a livestock farm. Summing up of the daily manpower requirement for various activates of the farm will provide you're the daily labour requirements of the farm and it will also helpful in daily allotment of labour for various works with efficiency.

Since the agriculture labour is a physical and straining work, an individual labour cannot be engaged seven days per week, he should be given two days rest per week. Considering that, an individual labour can be effectively allotted 20 days of work per month. In view of that, when a farm requires 10 man days per day for various activities, farm manager should have 15 (10 divide by 0.66) labours in the labour pool to allot 10 man-days per day with reasonable off time of two days per week.

Activity

1. Calculate the farm labour requirements per day of your farm
2. Forecast the one month labour requirement of your farm

Exam Corner

1. What is labour in agriculture?
2. What skilled and semi skilled labour?
3. What is unskilled labour in agriculture?
4. Functions of farm manager
5. What is labour forecast?
6. List the manpower requirements for agri activities?
7. How to work out the man days need of a day?
8. Labour requirements for dairy section

9. Labour requirements for piggery section
10. Labour requirements for sheep and goat section
11. Labour requirements for feed mills
12. How to calculate the labor pool for a month?

11

Organic Fodder Production

Learning Objectives

- Explain the concept of organic farming and its need
- Discuss the principles of organic farming
- Detail the various steps in organic fodder production

Food and Agriculture Organization defines organic agriculture is a unique production system which promotes and enhances agro-ecosystem health, including biodiversity, biological cycles and soil biological activity, and this is accomplished by using on-farm agronomic, biological and mechanical methods in exclusion of all synthetic off-farm inputs.

The beauty of organic agriculture production is dependency three elements namely soil, plants and animals. It is also called animal agriculture in which, animal depends on plants, plants depends on soil and soil depends on animals for their fertile life.

India, being a country with rich agricultural heritage, organic agriculture is not a new concept to us, it is our traditional and time tested method of agriculture using the principles of selecting indigenous crop varieties based on the soil type and season, use of farm based inputs, cyclical use of farm products, minimum dependency on external inputs and integrated farming approach etc. The overall objective of organic agriculture is cultivation of any crop with optimized yield in a sustainable way, by improving the soil health and eco systems and mitigating the environmental pollution.

Organic crop production is cultivating the crops under organic principles for human use and it is going in a long way in various parts of the world. On the other hand, organic fodder production relies on the same principles, in which cultivation of fodder is being carried out for the use of animals by applying the principles of organic agriculture for crop production and it is the basis for organic milk, egg and meat production.

Need of Organic Farming

Increase in population compels to stabilize agricultural production and productivity and there is a need to increase it further in sustainable manner. The agricultural production and productivity of Green Revolution with high external and chemical input use has reached a point after which diminishing return per unit area and soil ill health and environmental pollutions are negative outcomes. Thus, a balance needs to be maintained with minimum and renewable critical inputs for sustained production. Considering this issue, organic agriculture production principles are good choice of system in which production, productivity, safety, health can be ensured in crop and fodder production without any pollution to the environment, which can be called as Ever Green Revolution.

Key Principles of Organic Farming

1. Preserving the long term fertility of soils by maintaining sufficient organic matter in the soil, improving the soil biological activity, and careful mechanical intervention
2. Providing nutrients to the crop indirectly by using relatively insoluble nutrient sources, which are made available to the plant by the action of soil micro-organisms
3. Self-sufficiency of nitrogen in the soil is managed through the cultivation of legume crops in crop rotation and biological nitrogen fixation, use of green manures, use of organic materials including crop residues and livestock manures
4. Control of weed, disease and pest through crop rotations based on the soil type and season, natural predators, diversity, organic manuring, selecting resistant varieties and limited thermal, biological and chemical intervention
5. The extensive management of livestock in its eco system, and use of farm animal resources in a holistic way for reaping the mutual benefits for crop and animal production systems
6. Practicing crop and animal farming systems with minimum impact on environment and natural flora and fauna.

Organic Fodder Production

Organic fodder farming systems includes basic principles of organic farming which starts from conversion of land from conventional management to organic management. It consists of selection of suitable fodder varieties depending on the land soil and season, proper fodder crop rotation, use of organic manures, green manures, biological inputs in every stage fodder development including crop residue management. It also includes weeds and pest management by physical, cultural and biological methods and free of fertilizer and chemical application even in fodder preservation. Extensive management of livestock is integral approach which will improve the maintenance of biological cycles and as source of manure.

Fodder Field Management

The first step in organic fodder production is fodder field management in which tillage should be of minimum there by disturbance to the land should be minimum followed by application of organic manure like various composts, green manure and bio fertilizers like vermi compost to enrich the soil nutrient status and fertility.

Selection of Fodder Crops

Selection of fodder crops is a critical step in organic fodder production which depends on soil type, season and type of cultivation. Hybrid Cumbu Napier grass, multi cut fodder sorghum varieties and Desmanthus are good choices for irrigated farming in hot and dry climates for cut and carry system of feeding. Annual fodder sorghum and cowpea varieties are suitable in rain fed farming in tropical climates. Fodder maize and berseem are suitable for winter climates. Lucerne is suitable legume on cool climates for cut and carries system. Cenchrus and stylo are suitable choices for pasture establishment in hot and dry climates. Rhodes grass, Lucerne and white clover are choices for pasture in temperate climates.

Nutrient Management

In organic fodder production, nutrient management shall be through application of various organic manures, bio dynamic farming, use of bio fertilizers, vermi compost, coir compost and use of Panchakavya like products etc for needy nutrient availability and enhancement of soil activity and micro flora. Use of chemical fertilizers shall be strictly prohibited.

In organic fodder production apart from regular irrigation or rain feeding, catchment strips, contour bunds and summer ploughs are worth practices for rain water harvesting in the field itself. Organized farms can plan for micro irrigation system for water efficiency.

Weed control can be achieved by cover crop cultivation (ex. Growing cowpea in between maize or bajra), application of crop residue as mulch (Coir pith, paddy straw etc.) during the initial period of crop establishment which will reduces the weed competition and loss of water through evaporation for the improvement of microclimatic condition of the crop.

Plant Protection

In general fodder crops are pest and disease resistant. The strategy for the same includes selection of adaptive and resistant varieties, use of clean seed and planting material, use of suitable cropping system, use of balanced nutrient management, proper management techniques ie., avoid water stagnation with proper drainage system, proper selection of optimum planting time and spacing, use of proper sanitation measures etc. The common pests affecting the fodder are stem borer, leaf folder and sucking pest and disease. These insect and disease attaches can be controlled or by the application of neem oil based preparations and plant ashes.

Panchagavya

Panchagavya is a traditional organic formulation, made of chiefly five ingredients derived from cows. The name of the formulation indicates that it is a mix of five (Pancha) ingredients from cows (Gavya). The product is basically as Indian concoction with multi functions like nutrients supplements, pesticides, insecticides, growth promoter etc. and widely used in organic farming and fodder production. Use of Panchagavya also offers soil fertility and immunity to the plants against various diseases, there by improves the production potential.

Ingredients

1. Fresh cow dung - 10 kg
2. Cow urine - 10 lit
3. Cow milk - 2 lit
4. Cow curd - 2 lit
5. Cow ghee - 1 kg
6. Tender coconut water - 3 lit
7. Sugarcane juice - 3 lit
8. Ripened banana - 12 numbers
9. Yeast - 100 gm

Preparation Methodology

1. Mix thoroughly fresh cow dung (7kg.) + Cow ghee (1 kg.)
2. Incubate for 2 days
3. Add Cow urine (3 lit. + 10 lit of water)
4. Stir properly (morning and evening, daily for 1 week).
5. Add Sugarcane juice (3 lit.)
6. Add Cow milk (2 lit.)
7. Add Cow curd (2 lit.)
8. Add coconut water (3lit.)
9. Add yeast 100 gram and 12 ripened bananas
10. The whole mixture is to be incubated for two weeks and the preparation should be filtered through double layered muslin cloth
11. Stored in bottle under refrigerator and used as and when required. Sugarcane juice and coconut water are used to accelerate the fermentation which also help in minimizing the bad odour.

Properties of Panchagavya

Panchagavya contains several nutrients i.e. macronutrients like nitrogen, phosphorus, potassium and micronutrients which are required for the growth and development of plants and also contains various amino acids, vitamins, growth regulators like Auxins, Gibberellins and also beneficial micro organisms like Pseudomonas, Azotobacter and Phosphobacteria etc.

Dose of Panchagavya for Field Application

1. Spray method - Three per cent solution is effective. 3 litres of Panchagavya mixed with every 100 litres of water is suitable for all crops.
2. Flow system - The solution of Panchagavya can be mixed with irrigation water at 50 litres per hectare either through drip irrigation or flow irrigation.
3. Seed treatment: Three per cent solution of Panchagavya can be used to soak the seeds or dip the seedlings before planting. Soaking the seeds or dipping the seedlings for 30 minutes.

General Advantages of Panchagavya

Application of Panchagavya is organic and eco friendly in nature and it has multi functions like improving the soil fertility, improving immunity and growth promoting functions of the crop. It has some limitations like slow action, contamination in the fermentation process and lack of adoption. (*Source: TNAU- Agritech Portal*)

Uses of Organic Fodder Production

Organic fodder production forms the basis for the organic milk and meat production systems, and the marketing of those products are slowly getting momentum in Indian markets with premium price tag. However, organic fodder production mainly depends of animal based organic manure, for which integration animal component in crop farming is mandatory, but that component is often missing in intensive crop production. Moreover, organic manures are becoming costly due to low production and high demand. Conversion of conventional fodder farming system in to organic farming is a slow process and time consuming. Due to these factors, organic fodder production is slowly picking up in India, but sustained efforts will offer the benefits tangibly.

Activity

1. Design a model for organic fodder production for one acre of land and workout the inputs and budget for the same.
2. Prepare Panchagavya for your farm use

Exam Corner

1. Define organic agriculture
2. What is On farm and Off farm input?
3. What are the three elements of organic agriculture?
4. What is the need for organic farming?
5. Principles of organic farming
6. What is organic fodder production?
7. What is field management in organic farming?
8. How to select crops for organic farming
9. Nutrient management in organic farming
10. Plant protection in organic farming
11. Uses of organic fodder production
12. Scope of organic fodder production in future

12

Integrated Farming System

Learning Objectives

- Explain the concept and components of Integrated Farming System
- Discuss the functions of Integrated Farming System
- List the various models of Integrated Farming System

Integrated Farming System is a traditional concept in agriculture in which we are trying integrate various agriculture farming and its allied enterprises suitably for efficient use of single and multiple production function. In simple sense, it is a way integrating crop farming with livestock and poultry farming, fish farming, bee keeping and other agriculture technologies to enhance the value chain of farming system.

The core idea of integration is harvesting the complementary and supplementary relationship functions of various enterprises effectively and the art of using the waste of one enterprise to be the input of other enterprise. It is a efficient farming tool for small and marginal farmers to optimize the output per unit of land and investment. Moreover, it is more of organic, eco and soil friendly in nature.

Components of Integrated Farming Systems		
Agriculture components	**Livestock Components**	**Others**
Food crop	Dairy farming	Honey Bee keeping
Fruit crop	Sheep and Goat farming	Bio Gas production
Vegetable crop	Piggery farming	Vermi composting
Plantation crop	Poultry farming	Mushroom cultivation
Industrial & other crops	Fish farming	Organic growth promoters

Functions of Integrated Farming System

Productivity - Integration of crop and allied enterprises favours to increase economic yield per unit area, investment and time.

Profitability – Efficient use of biological cycles in the form of input and waste management, input cost is being decreases, there by profitability increases.

Sustainability – Integrated farming systems basically relies on farm based inputs and organic approach there by sustain the production systems with minimum cost and at the same time improves the soil health for overall productivity increase in a sustainable manner.

Balanced Food Production – Since integrated farming sytems produces various kinds of foods like cereals, pulses, fruits, vegetable, milk, meat, honey and others, it is producing balanced and nutritious food items for farmer's own use and end users.

Eco friendly - In integrated framing systems, biological cycles are well managed and art of using the waste is in practice. Out of the livestock and poultry, vermiculture, bio gas etc, waste is being effectively utilized by the farmers in the field itself and surplus is being sold for income. Based on that integrated farming system is more of organic in nature. Income throughout the year – Since IFS is linking the cropping with all the allied industries, there by producing various products thorough out the year, income all through the year from any one enterprise is ensured.

Models of Integrated Farming System	
1.	Paddy – Fish – Poultry
2.	Paddy – Fish – Vegetable
3.	Paddy – Fish – Piggery
4.	Coconut – Banana – Dairy – Vermicompost
5.	Coconut – Vegetable – Banana- Dairy- Vermicompost
6.	Coconut – Dairy – Poultry – Honeybee - Bio Gas
7.	Coconut –Dairy - Poultry – Hone bee – Vermicomposting
8.	Mango- Sheep and Goat- Honey bee
9.	Mango – Sheep and Goat- Poultry- Honey bee
10.	Timber trees – Poultry – Honey bee
11.	Timber trees – Fodder – Sheep and Goat – Honey bee
12.	Fruit trees – Timber trees – Poultry- Honey bee

Activity

1. Propose and design integrated farming system model suitable for your farm area
2. Design a suitable integrated farming system model for small ruminant production system.

Exam Corner

1. What is Integrated Farming System?
2. What are the two main components in IFS?
3. Characteristics of Integrated Farming System
4. List the agricultural components of IFS
5. List the animal components of IFS
6. List the other components of IFS
7. List the functions of IFS
8. What is productivity function of IFS?
9. What is sustainability function of IFS?
10. What is profitability function of IFS?
11. IFS and Balanced Food Production
12. List the models of Integrated Farming System

13

Registers Maintenance

Learning Objectives

- Discuss the role and functions of the registers in a farm
- List the registers to be maintained in a farm
- Explain the format of various registers of a farm

Register in general is recording of an event, transaction of stock and stores, money etc., and collectively it is aggregation of data. The farm will have lot of static and dynamic information and collection and recording all these information and storing the same is called register maintenance. Register maintenance is not a one time job, it is continuous process. Some of the registers will record the basic physical information and some other will record the financial transactions like expenditure, income etc. Maintenance of register with economics is more critical, because they decide profitability and economic efficiency of the farm. Registers are always associated with various activities carried out in a farm.

List of Registers			
1	Field Register	10	Weather Data Register
2	Open Well Register	11	Labour Register
3	Bore Well Register	12	Germination Register
4	Seed Stock Register	13	Sale Price Register
5	Fertilizer Register	14	Tree Register
6	Cropping Register	15	Non Expendable Article Register
7	Fodder Production Register	16	Expendable Article Register
8	Log Book for Vehicles	17	Condemned Article Register
9	Research Trials Register	18	Log Book for Power Generator

Field Register

This is a basic register in farm, which contains all the physical information of the farm like area of farm, coordinates, number of fields, fields numbers with area, type of land like irrigated or rainfed, farm ponds, water tanks, farm roads, office building details etc., However vital information of the field register is number of fields, type of land and its area. Farm map is basic part of field register, which will be useful for locating the existing physical structures and for future planning.

Open Well Register

This register will contain all the details about the open well available in the farm its field number, dimensions, details of motor pump installed and extent of area under irrigation. All the wells are to numbered serially and entered in to the register promptly.

Bore Well Register

This register will contain details about the list of borewells, its depth, motor pump installed and extent of area under irrigation.

Seed Stock Register

Seed stock register will record the details of the seed stock available in the farm, quantity of seasonal production and sales etc

Fertilizer Stock Register

Fertilizer stock register will have details of procurement of fertilizers, manures and related items and their issue details and balance stock details.

Cropping Register

The seasonal cropping details of the farm shall be recorded in the Cropping register for proper technical supervision and follow up. Cropping will be based on monsoon seasons and the same will be recorded in the register.

Fodder Production Register

Fodder production and issue to various sections of farm will be recorded on daily basis in the fodder production register. It will give a overall production potential and efficiency of the farm. Separate pages should be allotted to each fodder crop and monthly abstract should be arrived for over all supervision.

Log Book for Vehicles

Tractor, mini tractor, trailer, power tiller are the basic vehicles of the farm. Separate log book should be maintained in the form Part-1 and Part-2. Part-1 will contain hours of run, issue of fuel, overall efficiency of vehicle etc. Part -2 contains the repair and maintenance details of the vehicles.

Research Trials Register

Testing of new varieties of fodders and crops will be routine activity of a farm. Experimental design and units, data collected and results will be recorded systematically in this register to make a decision on scale up adoption.

Weather Data Register

On daily basis, weather variables like maximum and minimum temperature, relative humidity, wind velocity, sunshine hours, rainfall shall be recorded in the weather data register. Month wise averages shall be worked out for the same and may by published as bulletin for in house use.

Labour Register

Labour is a critical and costly input for agricultural operations. All the labour engagement details, number of labours for various activities, wage rates, payment details, attendance details etc shall be maintained in this register. Monthly abstract should be worked out to have control over cost on labour and to improve the labour efficiency. It will also helpful to forecast the labour requirement for future.

Germination Register

Fodder seed production is basic activity of livestock farm for their own use and sale. In both the cases, germination of the seed has to be assessed on batch wise and the details like batch number, quantity of seed produced, germination test details, methods and germination per cent should be recorded in the germination register to avoid future issues.

Sale Price Register

The products of the livestock farm are grouped in to two, livestock and agriculture products. To maintain the transparency in its sale process, Sale price of each product should be fixed at periodical interval by sale price fixation committee, generally once in year and the same should be recorded in the sale price register. Sale price may revised once in year or as and when the need arises by the appropriate committee as per the market price and demand for smooth and profitable sale.

Tree Register

Trees of the farm may be classified in to three multipurpose trees (Neem like trees), timber trees (Teak, Rose wood etc) and plantation trees (Coconut, Mango and Palmyrah etc.) . Mature trees of the same may counted in numbers and the same may entered in the tree register as per field numbers. The same may updated once in five years for effective inventory.

Non Expendable Article Register

Non expendable article register contains the list of all the non expendable article of the farm or otherwise called Dead stock of the farm. It means the article will be purchased once for regular use, and may not purchased once again, until the earlier one become unfit for use. All the agricultural implements, motors, tools, vehicles, and livestock farm equipments, lab equipments will come under this category. This register will contain the list of that article, its date of purchase, purchase value, depreciating rate, year wise depreciated value and current value etc. It should be updated once in year usually on first April of every year for effective inventory.

Expendable Article Register

This register contains all the expendable articles of the farm. It means the articles which are in regular use and repeat purchase like stationeries. Periodical purchase and issue details should be entered for record purpose.

Condemned Article Register

Condemnation of various old articles of the farm due to routine wear and tear is common activity. Based on the condemnation exercise may be carried out on annual basis by an appropriate committee and the list of condemned articles should be entered in the condemned article register for write off and auction.

Log Book for Power Generator

A separate log book should be maintained for power generator and it shall be divided in to namely Part -1 and 2. In Part-1, log of power generation operation like hours of run, fuel consumption may be recorded on daily basis and monthly abstract may worked out to arrive the hours of run per liter of fuel for effective decision making. In Part-2, spare parts replacement and service charges may be recorded.

Proper maintenance of registers is essential for any business; farm business is not an exception. The benefit of register maintenance is for effective decision making on various activities of the farm, based on the authenticated recordings.

Activity

1. Collect the data from the Field Register of your farm and calculate total area, cropped area, irrigated area, rain fed area, area of grass and leguminous fodder cultivation.
2. Collect the data from the Fertilizer Stock Register and workout the total quantity of various fertilizers used in a year and expenditure for the same.
3. Collect the data from the Fodder Production Register and calculate the total grass, leguminous and cereal fodder production in a year

   Collect the data from the Labour Register and calculate the labour requirements of your farm for a year and forecast the labour budget for the next year.

Exam Corner

1. Define register in agriculture farm?
2. What is the purpose of maintaining register?
3. List the various register of agriculture farm?
4. What is field register?
5. What is cropping register?
6. What is research trials register?
7. What is weather data register?
8. What is labour register?
9. What is germination register?
10. What is fodder production register?
11. What is a log book for tractor?
12. What is sale price register?

14

Economics of Fodder Production

Learning Objectives

- Discuss the role and functions of the registers in a farm
- List the registers to be maintained in a farm
- Design the format of various registers of a farm

Cost of production of fodder is critical in deciding the profitability of fodder production and livestock production. In intensive animal farming, fodder plays a vital, because of the reason that, most of the feeding regimen of dairy cattle, buffalo and small ruminant production system is fodder based. Fodder make out the bulk o feed expenditure apart from compounded feed. Understanding the economics of fodder production is vital in production of fodder in livestock farms.

Fodder production consists of various activities from preparation of field, tillage, manuring and fertilizing, sowing, irrigation, plant protection and harvest etc. Each of the activity involves costing based on the nature of activity and crop. Since the production system involves series of activities, standardizing the same with the allotment of costing is necessary for working out the economics. Addition of all costs involved in the production system will show the total production cost. Considering the average biomass yield for various crops, cost of production of fodder per unit may be arrived for working out the fodder cost in feeding regimen.

Technical Assumptions in Fodder Production	
1	**Cost of land preparation**
Cost of land preparation includes costs involved in various activities of land preparation like land leveling, tillage, bund, ridge or plot formation, rectification works etc. Ploughing charges and bund formation charges for tractor is Rs. 750 and Rs.500 per hour. Rectification charges are 10 man days per hectare at the wage rate of Rs. 436 per day per person.	
2	**Cost of seeds and sowing**
Cost of Lucerne, Sorghum and Desmanthus are Rs.600, Rs, 80 and Rs.550 per kg. Cost of Leucaena and Sesbania are Rs. 300 and Rs. 550 per kg. Cost of Hybrid Napier Grass is Re.1 per slip. Seed rate for Lucerne, Sorghum and Desmanthus is 15 kg, 40 kg and 20 kg per hectare respectively. Seed rate for Subabul and Sesbania is 7.5 kg and 10 kg per hectare. The seed rate of cow pea is 25 kg per hectare and the cost of seed is Rs.150 per kg. The seed for Maize is 40 kg per hectare and rate is Rs.50 per kg. The slip rate of hybrid Napier grass is 40000 slips per hectare with 20 per cent extra for replacement. Labour requirement for sowing is 15 man days per hectare.	
3	**Cost of manure and fertilizer**
The farm yard manure application as basal is for Lucerne, Maize and Hybrid Napier grass is 25 tonnes per hectare and for the other crops 12.5 tonnes per hectare. The cost of urea, SSP and MOP is Rs.5.50, Rs.5.25 and Rs.16 per kg respectively. Labour requirement is 10 man days per hectare for manure and 5 man days for fertilizer application	
4	**Cost of Weeding**
The labour requirement for weeding is 20 man days per hectare for single weeding. Perennial crops like Hybrid Napier and Desmanthus requires weeding and earthing up at the same labour input rate. A total of 3 weeding and 3 earthing up is required for Hybrid Napier and Desmanthus fodders. Sorghum and Maize requires one weeding as Annual crop.	
5	**Cost of irrigation**
Labour requirement is 2 man days per hectare. A total of 27 irrigations required with the gap 10 days excluding the two monsoon seasons for a period of 100 days.	
6	**Plant protection**
Generally fodder crops do not require plant protection. However, cost of plant protection for Lucerne and Sorghum assumed as Rs.1000 and Rs.500 respectively	
7	**Cost of harvest**
Labour requirement for harvest is 30 man days per hectare. Perennial crops like Hybrid Napier and Desmanthus requires seven harvests in a year. Cow requires 15 man days per hectare for harvest.	
8	**Green fodder yield**
Hybrid Napier grass -300 tonnes per hectare, Lucerne -80 tonnes per hectare Sorghum-40 tonnes per hectare, Desmanthus -80 tonnes per hectare Leucaena – 80 tonnes per hectare, Sesbania – 80 tonnes per hectare, Maize-40 tonnes	
Cost of production of each fodder is worked out based on the assumptions and average technical standards. It is only indicative in nature, cost may vary based on the input costs and green fodder yield from place to place.	

Economics of Grass Fodder Production for a year per hectare			
S. No.	Cost Items	Hybrid Napier grass	Guinea Grass
		Cost (Rs.)	
1	Cost of field preparation	13,290	11,110
2	Cost of seeds and sowing	58,900	56,720
3	Cost of manure, fertilizer and application	41,612	11,441
4	Cost of weeding and earthing up	52,320	17,440
5	Cost of irrigation	23,544	23,544
6	Cost of plant protection	1000	-
7	Cost of harvest	91,500	91,560
8	**Total Cost**	**2,82,126**	**2,11,815**
9	Green Fodder Yield (in tonnes)	300	150
10	**Cost of Production per kg of fodder**	**0.94**	**1.41**

Economics of Cereal Fodder Production per crop per hectare			
S.No.	Cost Items	Fodder Sorghum	Fodder Maize
		Cost (Rs.)	
1	Cost of field preparation	9860	11,110
2	Cost of seeds and sowing	9800	10,720
3	Cost of manure, fertilizer and application	25,665	23,307
4	Cost of weeding	8720	8720
5	Cost of irrigation	5232	6976
6	Cost of plant protection	500	-
7	Cost of harvest	13,040	13,080
8	**Total Cost**	**72,817**	**73,913**
9	Green Fodder Yield (in tonnes)	40	40
10	**Cost of Production per kg of fodder**	**1.82**	**1.84**

Economics of Leguminous Fodder Production for a year per hectare				
S. No.	Cost Items	Desmanthus	Lucerne	Cow Pea
		Cost (Rs.)		
1	Cost of field preparation	11,790	9610	9610
2	Cost of seeds and sowing	19,720	17,720	12,470
3	Cost of manure, fertilizer and application	25,999	26,694	13,344
4	Cost of weeding	26,160	17,440	8720
5	Cost of irrigation	32,264	23,544	4360
6	Cost of plant protection	1000	1000	500

7	Cost of harvest	76,300	65,400	6540
8	**Total Cost**	193233	161408	55,544
9	Green Fodder Yield (in tonnes)	125	80	20
10	**Cost of Production per kg of fodder**	1.54	2.01	2.77

Economics of Fodder Tree Production per year per hectare			
S. No.	**Cost Items**	**Leucaena**	**Sesbania**
		Cost (Rs.)	
1	Cost of field preparation	9610	11,110
2	Cost of seeds and sowing	9540	10,665
3	Cost of manure, fertilizer and application	4314	4313
4	Cost of weeding	8720	8720
5	Cost of irrigation	21,800	21,800
6	Cost of plant protection	-	1000
7	Cost of harvest	26,160	26,160
8	**Total Cost**	80,144	83,768
9	Green Fodder Yield (in tonnes)	80	80
10	**Cost of Production per kg of fodder**	**1.00**	**1.04**

Activity

1. Workout the cost of production of major fodders of your farm by collecting data from your farm registers and offers your comments.

Exam Corner

1. What is cost of production in agriculture?
2. List the activities of fodder production
3. What is fixed cost?
4. What is variable cost?
5. Explain the cost of land preparation
6. What is seed and sowing cost?
7. Detail the cost of manure and fertilizer
8. What is cost of weeding?
9. What is cost of irrigation?

10. What is cost of plant protection?
11. What is cost of harvest in fodder production?
12. Biomass yield and cost of production

15

Fodder Seed Production

Learning Objectives

- Explain the need for fodder seed production
- Discuss the practices of cereal and grass fodder seed production
- Discuss the practices of leguminous fodder seed production

Demand for fodder in intensive livestock farming necessitates the fodder seed production in all the livestock and fodder farms for their own use and sale to needy. In the recent past, fodder seed production is also becoming commercial activity of farmers as the income is promising. Since, there are number of new varieties of fodder are coming to the market, demand for their seed is also encouraging to produce the same commercially. Considering this, the farm managers should aware of fodder seed production technologies for cost effective and quality fodder seed production.

Cereal fodder – Fodder Sorghum – Seed Production

- Field preparation: Land should be free from volunteer plants
- Isolation distance: A distance of 400m is required for certified seed production since it is often cross pollinated crop
- Season : June-July and October – November
- Seed rate : About 5.0 kg is required for one hectare
- Spacing :45 X 15 cm
- Fertilizer dose: Recommended dose of NPK @ 100:50:50 kg / ha
- Harvest: Seeds can be harvested at physiological maturity on 45 days after 50% flowering.
- Seed treatment: Captan 75% WP at the rate of 70 g in 500 ml water for 100 kg of seed

- Storage: After seed treatment, the seed can be stored for one year in cloth bags and it the seeds need to be stored beyond one year, they should be dried to 8% moisture, treated and then stored in moisture vapour proof container like 700 gauge polythene bag.

Cereal fodder – Fodder Maize – Seed Production

- Field preparation : Land should be free from volunteer plants
- Isolation distance: A distance of 200 is required for certified seed production since it is often cross pollinated crop
- Season : June-July and October – November
- Seed rate : About 20.0 kg is required for one hectare
- Spacing : 60 X 20 cm
- Fertilizer dose: Recommended dose of NPK at the rate of 175 : 90 : 90 kg / ha
- Harvest: Seeds can be harvested at physiological maturity on 40 days after 50% flowering
- Seed treatment: Treat the harvested seeds with Captan 75%WP at the rate 2 g / kg plus Carbaryl at the rate of 200 mg / kg of seed
- Storage: After seed treatment, the seed can be stored for one year in cloth bags and it the seeds need to be stored beyond one year, they should be dried to 8% moisture, treated and then stored in moisture vapour proof container like 700 guage polythene bag.

Grass Fodder – Hybrid Napier – Slip Production

- Field preparation : Land should be free from volunteer plants
- Season : June-July and October – November
- Seed rate : About 40000 sett / ha is required for one hectare
- Spacing : 50 X 50 cm
- Fertilizer dose: Recommended dose of NPK at the rate of 150:50:40 kg / ha
- Harvest: Slips can be harvested at 80-90 days after planting

Grass Fodder – Guinea grass – Seed Production

- Field preparation : Land should be free from volunteer plants
- Isolation distance: A distance of 10m is required for certified seed production
- Seed rate : About 2.5 kg / ha is required for one hectare. Mechanical scarification for 2 minutes improves the seed germination by breaking dormancy
- Spacing :60 X 50 cm
- Fertilizer dose: Recommended dose of NPK @ 150:50:40 kg / ha
- Harvest: Seeds produced after first cut results in high quality seed. Seeds can be harvested after physiological maturity on 45 to 60 days after flowering

Leguminous Fodder – Desmanthus – Seed Production

- Field preparation : Land should be free from volunteer plants
- Pre-sowing treatment: Acid scarification with conc. Sulphuric acid at the rate of 200 ml / kg of seed for 5 minutes
- Seed rate : About 20 kg/ha is required for one hectare. Mechanical scarification for 2 minutes improves the seed germination by breaking dormancy
- Spacing : 60 X20 cm
- Fertilizer dose: Recommended dose of NPK @ 25:40:20kg/ha
- After first cut – 45:60:40 kg NPK/ha
- Foliar spray: Salicylic acid 200 ppm thrice after 50 % flowering at 10 days interval
- Harvest: Seeds can be harvested after physiological maturity on 35 days after flowering, when the pods turn brown and seeds become shiny brown
- Picking: Harvest the pods in different pickings
- Seed treatment: Treat the seed with diflubenzuron @2ppm as slurry treatment for scarified seeds and can be stored upto 12 months without viability loss

- Storage: Use gunny or cloth bags for short term storage with seed moisture content of 10% and use polylined gunny bag for medium term storage with moisture content 8%

Leguminous Fodder – *Stylo* spp. – Seed Production

- Field preparation : Land should be free from volunteer plants
- Isolation distance: About 25m for certified seed production
- Pre-sowing treatment: Acid scarification with conc. Sulphuric acid at the rate of 200ml / kg of seed for 4 minutes
- Seed rate: About 6.0 kg / ha is required for one hectare.
- Spacing :30 X 15 cm
- Fertilizer dose: Recommended dose of NPK @ 25:40:20 kg / ha
- Harvest: Seeds can be harvested after physiological maturity on 35 days after flowering
- Storage: Use gunny or cloth bags for short term storage with seed moisture content of 10 per cent and use polylined gunny bag for medium term storage with moisture content eight per cent.

Activity

1) Calculate the cost of fodder seed production of fodder Sorghum,
2) Calculate the cost of fodder seed production of Desmanthus
3) Calculate the cost of fodder slip production of hybrid Napier grass

Further Readings

Anil Kumar Singh, M.A.Khan, Nataraja Subash and Krishna Murari Singh. (2013). Forages and Fodder- Indian Perspective, Daya Publishing House. New Delhi.

Avatar Singh Bimbraw (2013). Production, Utilization and Conservation of Forage crops in India, Jaya publishing house, New Delhi.

Chandrasekaran. B, Annadurai, K. and Somadundram, E. (2010). A Text Book of Agronomy. New Age International Publishers, New Delhi.

Jayanthi.C., Vennila, C. and Devasenapathy, P. (2008). Farming System, Salish Serial Publishing House, New Delhi.

Pathak. N and H.C. Singh (2018). Fodder Production conservation and Evaluation for Livestock Production. Narendra Publishing House. New Delhi.

Raju R.A. (2018). Production Technology of Forage and Fodder crops. Agrobios (India), New Delhi.

Reddy.D.V. (2020). Fodder Production and Grassland Management, CBS Publishers and Distributors Private Limited, New Delhi.

Yellamanda Reddy. T. and G.H. Sankara Reddy (2015). Principles of Agronomy. Kalyani Publishers, New Delhi.

Annexures

Annexure-1: Conversion Table

Length	
1 mile	1.60 kilo metres
1 km	1000 metres
1 meter	100 centimetres
1 meter	3.28 feet
1 foot	12 inches
1 foot	30.48 centimetres
1 inch	2.54 centimetres
Area	
1 square kilo meter	100 hectare
1 hectare	2.47 acres
1 acre	4046 square meters
1 acre	100 cents
1cent	435.6 square feet
1 square meter	10.76 square feet
1 square foot	144 square inches
1 square foot	929 square centimetres
1 are	2.47 cents
Weight	
1 Tonne	1000 kilo gram
1 kilo gram	1000 grams
1 kilo gram	2.20 pounds
1 pound	0.45 kilograms
1 ppm	mg per kilogram
1 ppb	microgram per kilogram
Temperature	
Centigrade to Fahrenheit	^{o}C x 1.8 plus 32
Fahrenheit to Centigrade	(^{o}F minus 32) / by 1.8
Volume	
1 cubic meter	35.31 cubic feet
1 cubic foot	28 litres
1 cubic meter	1000 litres
1 TMC of water	2831 crores litre (apporx.)
Formulas	
Area of circle	Pi r^2
Volume of cylinder	Pi r^2h

Annexure-2: Sources for Fodder Crops Germplasm

Central Government	
1	Director, ICAR-Indian Grassland & Fodder Research Institute, Jhansi - 284003, India, Phone: 0510-2730666
2	The Officer In Charge, IGFRI- Regional Research Station, Dharwad (Karnataka) University of Agricultural Sciences (UAS) Campus,Dharwad, Karnataka- 580005
3	Officer In Charge , IGFRI – Hilly Regional Research Station , Srinagar, Jammu and Kashmir
4	Officer In Charge, IGFRI – Western Regional Research Station, Rajasthan – 304501
5	Director, Regional Station for Forage Production and Demonstration, Post Office Textile Mills, Hissar–125002, Haryana.
6	Director, In-charge, Regional Station for Forage Production and Demonstration, Avadi (Alamadhi) P.O. cattle farm, via Red Hills, Chennai-600052.
7	Director, In-charge, Regional Station for Forage Production and Demonstration, Pahadi Sharif, via Keshavgiri, Hyderabad–500 005, Andhra Pradesh
8	Director, In-charge, Regional Station for Forage Production and Demonstration, P.O. Netaji Subhas Sanatorium, Distt. Nadia, West Bengal-741 251
9	Director, Regional Station for Forage Production and Demonstration, Palej, Distt. Gandhinagar-382 355.
10	Director, In-charge, Regional Station for Forage Production and Demonstration, Suratgarh-335 804 Rajasthan.
11	Director, In-charge, Regional Station for Forage Production and Demonstration, Srinagar, Camp Office 599/A, Gandhinagar, Jammu-180 004.
12	Director, Central Fodder Seed Production Farm, Hessarghatta, Bangalore–560 088.
State Government	
13	Coordinator – Dhoni Farm, Kerala Livestock Development Board, Palakkadu – 678 009.
14	Professor and Head, Department of Forage Crops, Center for Plant Breeding and Genetics, Tamil Nadu Agricultural University Coimbatore – 641 003,Tamil Nadu.
15	Associate Professor and Head, Kkrishi Vigyan Kendra, Veterinary College and Research Institute campus, Namakkal - 637 002.
Private Firms	
16	• Mygrow Fodder Seeds, 10, Dr. Bhabha Road, Neemuch - 458441 (Madhya Pradesh, INDIA

Annexure-3: Register Format

Seed Stock Register								
Name of the Seed								
1	2	3	4	5	6	7	8	9
Date	Opening Balance	Receipt	Total	Issue	Transfer	CB	Sign	Remarks
Fertilizer Stock Register								
Name of the fertilizer								
1	2	3	4	5	6	7	8	9
Date	Opening Balance	Receipt	Total	Issue	Transfer	CB	Sign	Remarks
Expendable Article Register								
Name of the article								
1	2	3	4	5	6	7	8	9
Date	Opening Balance	Receipt	Total	Issue	Transfer	CB	Sign	Remarks
Fodder Production Register								
Name of the Fodder								
1	2	3	4	5	6	7	8	9
Date	Opening Balance	Receipt	Total	Issue	Transfer	CB	Sign	Remarks

<table>
<tr><th colspan="10">Log Book for Tractor / Trailer / Power Tiller</th></tr>
<tr><td>1</td><td colspan="2">2</td><td colspan="2">3</td><td>4</td><td>5</td><td>6</td><td>7</td><td>8</td></tr>
<tr><td></td><td colspan="2">Start</td><td colspan="2">Return</td><td rowspan="2">Hours of Run</td><td>Fuel Issue</td><td>Reading</td><td>Sign</td><td>Remarks</td></tr>
<tr><td>Date</td><td>Time</td><td>Opening Reading</td><td>Time</td><td>Closing Reading</td><td></td><td></td><td></td><td></td></tr>
</table>

<table>
<tr><th colspan="10">Log Book for Power Generator – Part- 1</th></tr>
<tr><td>1</td><td colspan="2">2</td><td colspan="2">3</td><td>4</td><td>5</td><td>6</td><td>7</td><td>8</td></tr>
<tr><td rowspan="2">Date</td><td colspan="2">On</td><td colspan="2">OFF</td><td rowspan="2">Hours of Run</td><td>Fuel Issue</td><td>Reading</td><td>Sign</td><td>Remarks</td></tr>
<tr><td>Time</td><td>Opening Reading</td><td>Time</td><td>Closing Reading</td><td></td><td></td><td></td><td></td></tr>
</table>

<table>
<tr><th colspan="8">Tree Register</th></tr>
<tr><td colspan="8">Date of Survey:</td></tr>
<tr><td>Field No.</td><td></td><td>Area</td><td></td><td>Type of Land</td><td></td><td colspan="2"></td></tr>
<tr><td>Sl.No.</td><td>Tree No.</td><td>Girth in cms</td><td>Type of Tree</td><td colspan="4">Remarks</td></tr>
<tr><td></td><td></td><td></td><td></td><td colspan="4"></td></tr>
<tr><td></td><td></td><td></td><td></td><td></td><td></td><td></td><td></td></tr>
<tr><td colspan="8">Tree Register may be maintained field wise and abstract may be made field and type of tree wise. Survey may be taken once in three years.</td></tr>
</table>

Germination Register					
Name of the seed					
Field No.		Batch No.		Batch Qty.	
Test Method and Date					
Result:					
Remarks:					

Condemned Article Register								
List of condemned article						Year		
1	2	3	4	5	6	7	8	9
Sl. No.	Name of the Article	Quantity	Page No. of Non Expend-able article Register	Date of Purchase	Value at the time of Pur-chase	Date of Con-demna-tion	Value at the time of Con-demna-tion	Remarks

Field Register				
Type of land	Irrigated / Rain fed		Year	
Sl.No.	Field No.	Area	Type of crop	Remarks

Open Well Register				
Year				
Sl.No.	Well No.	Field No.	Dimension	Details

Bore Well Register				
Year				
Sl.No.	Bore Well No.	Field No.	Depth	Details

Weather Data Register							
Year					Month		
Date	Day Temperature	Max. Temperature	Min. Temperature	Relative Humidity	Wind speed	Sun shine hours	Rain fall

Labour Register			
Year		Date	
Date	Activity	Number of labour allotment	Remarks
1			
2			
	Total		

Annexure-4

Sl.No.	List of fodder and multipurpose trees		
1	Acacia spp.	11	*Morus indica*
2	Adina cordifolia	12	*Moringa oleifera*
3	Albizia spp	13	*Petrocarpus marsupium*
4	Atrocarpus	14	*Sesbania grandiflora*
5	Azadirachta indica	15	*Sesbania sesban*
6	Dalbergia sissoo	16	*Tamarindus indica*
7	Glyricidia sepium	17	*Tectona grandis*
8	Hardwickia binata	18	*Thespesia populnea*
9	Leucaena leucocephala		

Index